Theology and
Catholic Higher Education

Theology and Catholic Higher Education

Beyond Our Identity Crisis

Massimo Faggioli

ORBIS BOOKS

Maryknoll, New York 10545

Founded in 1970, Orbis Books endeavors to publish works that enlighten the mind, nourish the spirit, and challenge the conscience. The publishing arm of the Maryknoll Fathers and Brothers, Orbis seeks to explore the global dimensions of the Christian faith and mission, to invite dialogue with diverse cultures and religious traditions, and to serve the cause of reconciliation and peace. The books published reflect the views of their authors and do not represent the official position of the Maryknoll Society. To learn more about Maryknoll and Orbis Books, please visit our website at www.orbisbooks.com

Manufactured in the United States of America.
Manuscript editing and typesetting by Joan Weber Laflamme.

Library of Congress Cataloging-in-Publication Data

Names: Faggioli, Massimo, author.
Title: Theology and Catholic higher education : beyond our identity crisis / Massimo Faggioli.
Description: Maryknoll, New York : Orbis Books, [2024] | Includes bibliographical references and index.
Identifiers: LCCN 2024017953 (print) | LCCN 2024017954 (ebook) | ISBN 9781626985841 (trade paperback) | ISBN 9798888660393 (epub)
Subjects: LCSH: Catholic universities and colleges—History—20th century. | Catholic Church—Education—History—20th century. | Theology—Study and teaching—Catholic Church—History—20th century. | Catholic universities and colleges—History—21st century. | Catholic Church—Education—History—21st century. | Theology—Study and teaching—Catholic Church—History—21st century.
Classification: LCC BX922 .F34 2024 (print) | LCC BX922 (ebook) | DDC 378/.0712—dc23/eng/20240527
LC record available at https://lccn.loc.gov/2024017953
LC ebook record available at https://lccn.loc.gov/2024017954

*I dedicate this book to
the incredibly vital and dedicated world
of Catholic higher education,
my adoptive alma mater*

Contents

Editorial Note

This book is the result of reflections resulting from my teaching experience, scholarly writing, service in the university and in academic organizations, and public scholarship for a larger audience. Some of the chapters in this book utilize material that was initially proposed in shorter articles and essays published in various languages over several years.

The content of these articles and essays has been thoroughly expanded, updated, and in some cases revised in its substance, orientation, and conclusions.

"A Wake-Up Call to Liberal Theologians," *Commonweal* online, March 6, 2018.

"Catholic Universities Not Doing Enough to Address the Sex Abuse Crisis," *La Croix International*, April 9, 2019.

"Endangered Species. Is There a Future for Lay Catholic Theologians?" *Commonweal* online, December 17, 2018.

"The Great Displacement of Theology: Where Is the Future of 'Faith Seeking Understanding'?" *La Croix International*, March 23, 2023.

"Hierarchy and Theology Alike Are Caught Up in Catholic Disruption," *National Catholic Reporter*, June 7, 2019.

"Ohne Tradition kein Fortschritt: Wie sich die kirchliche Lehre weiterentwickeln kann," *Herder Korrespondenz* 9/2023, 26–29.

"Opposition to Pope Francis Is Rooted in a Rejection of Vatican II," *National Catholic Reporter*, April 4, 2022.

"Il sapere religioso in occidente," in *Fare teologia per questo mondo, per questo tempo*, Associazione Teologica Italiana, Atti del Congresso di Napoli 2021, 25–46, Milano: Glossa, 2022.

"La teologia nelle università cattoliche, tra orizzonte post-ecclesiale e paradigma tecnocratico," *Studia Patavina* 69 (2022/1): 19–30.

Introduction

The Great Displacement of Theology

As a lay Catholic theologian and historian, I'm fortunate to be a professor in a department of theology and religious studies in a Catholic university in the United States. I moved from Europe to the United States in 2008 in order to teach. I love having the opportunity to teach undergraduate students theology. Often the course fulfills a core requirement and they have little or no pre-existing interest on the lay level in the discipline when it doesn't directly relate (as they see it) to their area of interest. Before Vatican II that would have been unthinkable. The development of the postconciliar period since the late 1960s has transformed the way we do theology. But the future of the discipline is very uncertain. Not only the discipline, but the future of the *universitas* as such is in doubt.

Recent cuts in theology programs decided by university administrators have rattled the community of Catholic theologians in the United States and in the Anglo-American world. It is now a familiar story—a board of trustees of Catholic colleges and universities voted to cut not only the theology department, but often also the liberal arts programs. In many instances courses in these fields are no longer offered as majors, although some of them remain part of the university's course offerings in a liberal arts core curriculum.

These cuts often follow a restructuring of the university's focus during previous academic years. It is not just the board of trustees; in some cases restructuring of the core curriculum at the expense of the requirement of theology courses and the liberal arts is fueled by a suspicion of the true value of these disciplines or by a lack of interest by faculty and administrators in other departments of these Catholic colleges and universities.

Especially in the United States it is the brave new world of higher education that now is transforming the unparalleled, large network of Catholic colleges and universities that Catholicism created. Cutting previously required courses in the liberal arts is among the steps taken toward selling out to technocracy. That is not something only administrators can be blamed for. In many Catholic universities, *aggiornamento*—updating—and changes related to the study of theology have ceded ground to non–Vatican II or anti–Vatican II cultures: often, theology has fallen into the hands of the traditionalists without offering any alternative vision for the field, as theologians who are non-traditionalists harbor the illusion that it is a marketing problem and not a product problem.

What happened at these colleges is a story that has repeated itself across the country in recent years: Catholic colleges and universities that compete in a market-oriented system are cutting their theology programs in favor of more "professionalizing" courses. In part, this is due to the undeniable lack of majors and minors in institutions that have become extremely expensive to attend—where theology is seen as a luxury, a nonessential field among other, more practical ones. But there is also a fundamental lack of faith in the liberal arts and theology held by many in the new cohort of lay (non-clergy, non-religious) administrators running Catholic colleges and universities these days.

This is not new. The role of theology in the institutions of education has changed before. In the first centuries of the Common Era, an "episcopal-monastic theology" took the form of biblical commentaries. At the beginning of the second millennium the model shifted toward a "university theology," which became the queen of the disciplines within the newborn universities.

Theologians became professional intellectuals focused on theological questions framed with a very complex philosophical language, taking the truths uncovered by philosophers such as Aristotle and seeking to show how those truths are compatible with the Christianity of European Christendom.

Today the role of theology in the university is part of the legacy—or the remains—of that nineteenth-century model of the German university. Catholic institutions in the United States adapted that model, together with the preexisting seminary system, for the formation of ministers, in order to serve the sons and daughters of the "immigrant church" who were in need of an education on a par with offerings at Protestant universities and public schools.

This higher education system ran parallel to the structure of the Catholic Church, centered on the hierarchical role of the bishops and the superiors of the religious orders, and the inexpensive labor—the ministry—of the members of the clergy, the religious, and the nuns. Now disappearing, at least in the West, that system is meeting a time of the great displacement of academic theology. It is not clear where, if, or how it will survive except in a handful of large and endowed universities that are not representative of the whole fabric of Catholic institutions.

This is also a great moment of crisis, for among some of the achievements from the Second Vatican Council (1962–65) and the post–Vatican II period, theology finally started to be taught not just by male celibate clergy, but also by lay men and women. Another achievement of the post–Vatican II period was that Catholic theology was no longer practiced largely in Europe and the Western world, but also in the Global South—Latin America, Africa, and Asia. The disestablishment of academic theology from

Catholic universities in the Anglo-American world will *not* always help the growth of new global Catholic voices.

There is the temptation to look at the changes as the inevitable result of secularization in the Western world: a shrinking church membership and the expansion of Catholic higher education from smaller colleges to universities offering a range of professional programs. These do factor into how secularization has changed Catholic colleges and universities, but there are other factors to take into account. We live in a different world now, no longer the world of bourgeois capitalism but of technocratic globalization. The ethos of the modernizing bourgeoisie centered on the concepts of civilization (*Kultur*) and formation (*Bildung*) as necessary for reshaping a social and political system where knowledge (*Wissenschaft*) was important for the economy, but also for the formation to citizenship and public opinion. The technocratic ethos of the current generation is not often convinced of the importance of a well-rounded education. The critical thinking that one develops by grappling with questions concerning religion and faith is not seen as relevant. More so, it is often perceived as the enemy of the technocratic world.

The ongoing great displacement of theology carries many unknowns. But as we've seen, this cannot be blamed entirely on the institutional church. In many Catholic universities founded by religious orders and clergy, the old leadership has been replaced by lay leaders. Replacing the clergy with lay leadership is no guarantee of a Catholic theological ethic. And the institutional church seems to have little to say about the shift in leadership. This estrangement between Catholic universities and the hierarchical church means that bishops are unable or possibly unwilling to effect larger changes related to theology in higher education.

The marginalization of theology from the university is a significant problem for the church as a whole, and not just for those who have lost or will lose their jobs in academia or for the students who will no longer be offered a wider range of theological and humanities courses. It also a step backward from the rise of democratization of theology faculty over the last fifty years, which included Catholic women teaching theology in Catholic institutions. And for the often self-trained and self-appointed fortunetellers masquerading as theologians or church experts all over the internet, this is considered a victory. These self-appointed voices harbor a re-clericalization of the thinking of the church. But the changes also reveal the betrayal of the promise made by Catholic schools to students, their families, and the whole ecclesial community, to provide an education to develop whole human beings, an education where the problem of God and faith is taken seriously as part of the whole person.

This raises further serious questions, especially given the situation of the Catholic Church today. If theology and the education of the whole person are being diminished, how can the work of theology, of ethics, of the humanities, of the church take place on critical issues such as the abuse crisis? How is it possible to be a discerning church if we keep eliminating theology from Catholic higher education, thus accelerating the disappearance of public engagement by and with the church?

The fundamental questions about the place of Catholic theology today include these: Where can theology be taught and studied in the church? Where can it be taught and its importance understood in the public square? Not asking these questions at a basic level means we are at the cusp of a long-term intellectual disaster for the Catholic mind. And this is not just a problem for those working in academia: professors, students, administrators, donors.

Will theology be relegated to small pockets of academia now? Will theology be possible outside academia in any engagement with public life? Will Catholic colleges and universities be *Catholic* without a visible presence of theology?

Each troubling question leads to another. But perhaps a more troubling question is, can one be a theologian *inside* Catholic academia today? The inquisition that academic theologians working in market-oriented universities fear the most these days is not the Holy Office in the Vatican, but the office run by lay technocrats independent from ecclesiastical authority, yet very much dependent on other, less visible and identifiable, powers. Despite all the DEI (diversity, equity, and inclusion) initiatives, the disappearance of theology will make our Catholic campuses less diverse and inclusive. It will also make them less Catholic and less well rounded.

This book begins with this growing set of interlinking questions. Each chapter will look at different questions and considerations. Here is a basic overview: In the first chapter we'll look at the frame of the identity crisis of Catholic higher education in the context of the massive changes in the ecclesial and theological conversations since the time of Vatican II. The second chapter analyzes the interruption and major source of disconnect between the university and the church in the theological reception of Vatican II. The third chapter focuses on the shifting position and marginalization of theology within Catholic higher education. The fourth chapter looks at some consequences of these developments in the formation of Catholics (not only of those in ministry) for a synodal church. The fifth chapter looks at the role and responsibility of Catholic theology in the wider society, the academy, and the church. And in the concluding pages, I advance some proposals for addressing the current identity crisis.

I believe this book comes at an important time in the life of the church, that is, in the context of the "Synodal Process" begun in 2021 and its reception. In this global ecclesial conversation the voice of Catholic colleges and universities has been noticeable for their marginalized role, with some notable exceptions, including preparation between 2021 and 2023 with the United States, as the largest network in the world of Catholic higher education. Their role was marginal not just due to deep-seated fears in the Vatican of the risk of injecting elitist concerns and academic jargon into the delicate process of ecclesial discernment. This marginality speaks also to the strange, strained, and dangerous relations between the church and Catholic higher education today.

In these last two decades, as a member of both academia and the church in the United States, I have been brought into this universe of vocation and mission to be an educator, to meet the conversation of theology and education with the life of these academic communities of people and places, with their classrooms, offices and hallways, libraries, cafeterias, and chapels. This book serves as part of my work and reflection on the urgency of theological education. I offer this book from my particular location as someone who grew up Catholic but didn't have a Catholic education in a Catholic school. In Italy, I went to public schools, which in the seventies and eighties were a peculiar mixture of confessional state and anticlericalism. In high school, for example, we studied Latin and Greek for five years and read Virgil and Homer in the original, even as the Bible was absent from the canon of texts accepted as part of the classical tradition.

Then I was hired by a Catholic higher education institution to develop Catholic education, theological education, at the university level. This vocation has also served as a wake-up call for me—and I hope for those reading this book—against any sense of both complacency and inevitability vis-à-vis the huge changes in this time of transition in the history of colleges and universities.

1

Recognizing the Identity Crisis

The Remains of Previous Eras

What Remains of the Post–Vatican II Period

One popular way to explain the source of the crisis of Catholic theology today—within and beyond the university system—is to blame the post–Vatican II pontificates from Paul VI to Benedict XVI for their failure to receive adequately the theological and doctrinal developments of the council. This explanation, however, leaves out those ways in which academic theologians have received and implemented Vatican II in their institutions of higher education and learning. What resulted is an ongoing estrangement between academic theology and the church.

This estrangement is one reason numbers of younger, militant Catholics are now turning to neo-traditionalist circles for their education. This new generation is reexamining what's happened in the church since the 1960s and reacting against the theology that came out of the Second Vatican Council. Some younger Catholics are also questioning the legitimacy of the secular, pluralistic state in this *Zeitgeist*, fascinated by the rise of post-liberal, anti-liberal, and illiberal political theories and theologies.

The concerns of academic theology, and especially *Catholic* theology with the development of Catholic social teaching after Vatican II on relations between the church and political modernity, are no longer solely academic concerns, as they affect the future of our societies.

Those who have contact with these young Catholics—for example, college students—may have noticed that this wave of theological traditionalism, this quest for continuity to the exclusion of the dynamic character of the tradition, is not just "trad" ideas coming from a few marginal intellectuals. Catholic anti-liberalism is part of a broader phenomenon, a new quest for Catholic identity that takes various expressions—liturgical, doctrinal, political, and educational.

This rise of anti-*aggiornamento* Catholicism marks a regression in the ability of some Catholics in higher education to understand our age. But it also says something about the state of Catholic theology, especially in the Anglo-American world, and how much has changed since Vatican II. Especially in the American system, where there is no constitutionally established church, academic theology is part of a religious and ecclesial Catholic establishment. But we are seeing that the institutions that support academic theology will not last forever. And for Catholic academic theology to be healthy, it cannot depend entirely on a few great institutions; it also needs the many smaller Catholic colleges, many of which now struggle to stay open. A related issue within Catholic schools is also the shrinking pool of prospective students.[1] The fate of Catholic theology in the Western world is inseparable from the fate of academic theology, which in turn depends on universities, but also a wider sphere of publishers, academic journals, magazines, grade schools, and seminaries. One can perhaps imagine the church surviving

---

[1] See Kevin Carey, "The Incredible Shrinking Future of College," *Vox*, November 21, 2022.

intellectually without academic theology, but it would be the poorer for losing that resource, challenge, conversation partner, and intellectual accountability partner.

What the wave of anti-*aggiornamento* pushback does tell us is that something has been happening to Catholic theology and religious-studies departments. Important to this change is one particular document in recent history regarding church teaching. In 2018, Philadelphia Archbishop Charles Chaput responded to a question following his Villanova University lecture. Someone asked him to speak about the role of John Paul II's apostolic constitution *Ex Corde Ecclesiae* (1990) in Catholic universities today.[2] He answered that the document issued by the US bishops in 1999 to implement *Ex Corde* "had no teeth." This was as frank an acknowledgment of the estrangement between Catholic theologians and the church as one could ask for.

The post–Vatican II period emancipated theology from ecclesiastical control, but it also emancipated the Catholic Church from academic theology. A first series of tensions surfaced in the 1960s: the rector of Catholic University of America barred four progressive theologians from speaking in 1963; that same year, the Congregation for Seminaries and Universities quietly issued a decree that all honorary degrees awarded by Catholic universities had to be approved by the Holy See. This prompted an impassioned defense of institutional autonomy by Cardinal Francis Spellman of New York; in 1963, St. John's University in New York fired thirty-one faculty in the name of preserving the institution's basic religious character, violating academic due process and setting off a faculty strike; Archbishop Karl Alter of Cincinnati intervened in a University of Dayton conflict over a philosophy professor accused of heresy; and, of course, the first Charles Curran case at Catholic University of America for his

---

[2] For the lecture, see Charles Chaput, "Things to Come: Faith, State, and Society in a New World," *The Catholic World Report*, February 22, 2018.

positions on questions of sexual ethics, in 1967 (even before the publication of Paul VI's encyclical *Humanae Vitae* in 1968).[3]

Another set of breakdowns between bishops and theologians throughout the late 1970s and early 1980s had to do with the theology of sexuality. But the schism spread to other subjects with damage that hardly made viable the very idea of the mission of theology in its relationship to the church. The Catholic ground for the "culture wars" had been prepared.

In 1979, a letter from the Congregation for the Doctrine of the Faith criticized *Human Sexuality: New Directions in American Catholic Thought*, a study commissioned by the Catholic Theological Society of America.[4] Bernard Law, who was appointed Archbishop of Boston in 1984, publicly criticized Cardinal Joseph Bernardin's Common Ground initiative, an effort to build bridges between different elements of the US church, including academic theologians.[5] Then between the mid-1980s and 1992 the controversy about the new catechism arose. Many theologians feared their critical academic work was being reduced to catechesis; some also worried that the catechism was nullifying

---

[3] In 1954, a confrontation with Cardinal Alfredo Ottaviani, pro-prefect of the Vatican Congregation of the Holy Office over a book chapter by John Courtney Murray, SJ, was particularly formative for Fr. Theodore Hesburgh, president of the University of Notre Dame. See Edward P. Hahnenberg, "Theodore M. Hesburgh, Theologian: Revisiting Land O' Lakes Fifty Years Later," *Theological Studies* 78, no. 4 (2017): 930–59. See also Mark S. Massa, *The Structure of Theological Revolutions: How the Fight over Birth Control Transformed American Catholicism* (New York: Oxford University Press, 2018); id., *The American Catholic Revolution: How the Sixties Changed the Church Forever* (New York: Oxford University Press, 2010).

[4] See *Human Sexuality: New Directions in American Catholic Thought*, ed. Anthony Kosnik (New York: Paulist Press, 1977); Sacred Congregation for the Doctrine of the Faith (prefect cardinal Franjo Seper), "Letter to Archbishop John R. Quinn, President of the National Conference of Bishops in the USA," July 13, 1979.

[5] See Steven P. Millies, *Good Intentions: A History of Catholic Voters' Road from Roe to Trump* (Collegeville, MN: Liturgical Press, 2018).

the teachings of Vatican II by forcing them into a conservative mold.

All these developments led to more separation between academic theology and church hierarchy. Today, few Catholic theologians in academia also advise their local bishop or help the bishops' conference draft its statements. This lack of contact with the leadership of the church is far-ranging, including affecting our ability to develop academic programs that educate Catholic lay ministers, parish and school staff, and those working in social agencies and hospitals.

One of the paradoxical effects of post–Vatican II is that the work of Catholic theologians has become less and less important to many Catholic leaders (bishops, public intellectuals, big donors), who instead have turned their attention to initiatives that address the "culture wars."

But even apart from ideology, there was a real turn away from contemporary Catholic *theology* toward Catholic *culture*. This meant that many Catholic students, especially in America, learned about Catholicism not from theology professors, but from Catholic professors of literature, the arts, history, and politics. While these students likely do not appreciate the importance and coherence of theological thinking as such, the cultural, rather than theological, understandings fail to address the bigger issues.

The influence of the Catholic intellectual tradition on all the disciplines, not just theology, is one of the themes of *Ex Corde Ecclesiae*. But to many, this meant that one could get a Catholic education without studying much—or indeed any—Catholic theology. Because of the left-right split that widened during the pontificate of John Paul II, many Catholics, including intellectuals and even academics, wrote theology off as a discipline corrupted by liberal opinion. Catholic scholars of literature, art, history, and other disciplines could teach a kind of Catholic studies that focused on the high cultural ideals of the Christian West and largely ignored or rejected post-conciliar theology. That meant the growing polarization in the United States between left and right in theology during the years of John Paul II, and especially since the 1990s, relegated Catholic theology in universities to being the handmaiden of political progressivism.[6]

As a consequence, this allowed not only Catholic seminaries for the formation of future priests to present themselves as *the* Catholic alternative to academic theology, but also allowed higher-education professors of literature, art, history, law, and business on the neo-conservative or traditionalist side to claim a form of Catholic intellectual tradition that is independent and opposed to academic theology, identifying themselves as Catholic because they represented and re-proposed the high cultural ideals of the Christian West that progressivism abandoned.

Note that some of the most prominent young commentators on current Catholic affairs have little formal theological formation, even though they may be informed about aspects of the Catholic intellectual tradition. This can be traced back to the mutual estrangement between the church and Catholic theological education. At the very moment many Catholic colleges and universities were freed from episcopal interference, they happily surrendered to the influence of corporate donors eager to fund conservative projects on Catholic campuses—projects that often combined theological traditionalism with neo-liberal or libertarian economic ideology.

This neo-Catholic intellectual elite inherited and cultivated over time strong ties with the political and economic-financial establishment that in the United States was looking for a new,

---

[6] "Political theology's usual way of bringing temporality to the fore is to insist on an eschatological interpretation of God's salvific justice as the response to suffering, oppression, and hopelessness. . . . As important and as moving as this insight has been, though, it can no longer alone do the job of engaging a presentist culture of anxious inertia." Anthony J. Godzieba, "Who Is the 'Polis' Addressed by Political Theology? Notes on a Conundrum," *Theological Studies* 80, no. 4 (2019), 891–92.

politically reliable, conservative Christian identity, at a time when the tradition of the mainline Protestant churches, which had innervated the country since its foundation, was falling apart intellectually and fragmenting sociologically. In a perverse reversal of fortunes, soon after academic theology freed itself from the surveillance of ecclesiastical hierarchies, a new *captivitas* began in the hands of "Big Business," happy to donate money to conservative or traditionalist Catholic projects on college campuses and Catholic universities: theological traditionalism and apologetic literature, accompanied by a neo-liberal economic ideology.

The Catholic intellectual crisis is at the root—not just an aspect—of the political crisis of the West. The revolt of illiberal populism is nourished by the emerging talents of the religious right, including the Catholic right, and has entered the cultural and academic mainstream from graduates of Ivy League universities, Catholic intellectuals who studied Hobbes and Tocqueville with generous scholarships through study centers at the service of politics and financed by big money. Reactionary Catholicism represented by this new fabric of cultural institutions is predominantly political, aimed at professionals of the political-legal-economic complex, and has little background or interest in the disciplines of the intellectual canon that form the Catholic tradition.[7]

This phenomenon should be a wake-up call for Catholic theologians in America and beyond, posing a challenge to the post–Vatican II academic-theological complex of research and teaching institutions of Catholic theology. In the long term it will threaten the intellectual vitality, if not the very survival, of academic theology at Catholic colleges and universities.

---

[7] A classic is Yves Congar, *Tradition and Traditions: An Historical and a Theological Essay* (New York: Macmillan, 1967). In today's theological conversations the work of Congar, the most important theologian at Vatican II, receives much less attention compared to other giants of the twentieth-century Catholic intellectual tradition.

In light of this present post–Vatican II moment, theologians and religious-studies scholars teaching in Catholic universities face two immediate issues. The first relates to the *canon*. Is there a canon of theology on Catholic campuses in America, or do we now have so many canons that the very idea of a canon has been lost? With Catholic theology in America being displaced by other voices claiming to represent Catholic culture, should theologians have a clearer sense of what theology at a Catholic university ought to include? Even as these questions are being asked, tradition-focused students and professors who reject or ignore post-conciliar theology have certainly established a replacement canon that is well-defined, if by nothing else, by the rejection of Vatican II and post–Vatican II theology. But for those seeking theological scholarship and academic vitality, there is no clear canon of non-traditionalist Catholic theology. In academic jargon, a more "capacious" idea of Catholic theology often means less Catholic and less theological. Syllabi usually become a compromise between what those teaching theology are personally invested in teaching (perhaps related to their own research projects) and what courses and course materials students are willing to invest time in—as the credibility of theology departments depends in part on their ability to get a sufficient number of students to major or minor in theology.

That leaves too many theology departments trying to remain "relevant" by offering courses I believe will ultimately make theology less relevant. The current anxiety in academia for relevance means that Catholic theology is often reduced to Catholic social teaching, which, as fundamental and important as it is, doesn't reflect the full range of theological explorations and is more likely to reveal an understanding of our world typical of the mass society and industrial capitalism that reveres our "society of singularities," our "performance society."[8]

---

[8] See Byung-Chul Han, *Vita Contemplativa: In Praise of Inactivity*, trans. Daniel Steuer (Medford, MA: Polity, 2024), 76.

At the same time, the growing irrelevance of academic theology is the result of a long line of *aggiornamento* Catholic theologians who believed *aggiornamento* theology did not need to be defended because it was self-evident. This has resulted in many Catholic students choosing instead to major or minor in "Catholic Studies," as progressive Catholic students major in "Justice and Peace Studies" or similar programs. For students, theology is simply less appealing.

The second problem comes from the lack of *ecclesial commitment*—where both church leaders and theologians are unaware that the Catholic academic complex also has a place *within* the church, even if its integrity requires a certain intellectual independence. Theology needs the church as much as the church needs theology. Today, most members of the hierarchy have not studied at a secular university, and lay theologians seldom have the same *kind* of theological training their bishops have. Not surprisingly, each feels alienated from the other. But the institutional church has a resilience to the vicissitudes of history that Catholic academia on its own likely does not. Even post–Vatican II the institutional church can ignore market forces in a way that academia cannot. Reintegrating academic theology with the rest of the church is made complicated by the choice of departments of theology—the well-formed choice, which should not be reversed, but creates a widening gap even so—to make departments of theology and religious studies on Catholic campuses more diverse through the hiring of non-Catholic professors.

But ecclesial commitment is not merely about active membership in the church. At a minimum, theologians and religious-studies professors should be more aware of their duty to respond to questions that traditionalist or conservative Catholic students have and for which they often find no answer in liberal-progressive theology departments. Committed Catholic undergrads pick up on the intra-Catholic ideological battles that faculty may be responding to in research and the politics of college departments and come away with the impression that the Catholic faculty in theology and religious-studies departments are anti-Catholic or somehow hostile to the faith and the church they know and grew up with.

Theologians and religious-studies professors teaching on Catholic campuses ignore at their own peril the seismic shifts happening in church politics and in the relationship between the institutional church and Catholic higher education. In our twenty-first-century post–Vatican II world, Catholic theologians need to offer an alternative to the current neo-traditionalist vision of the Catholic tradition. In order to do that, we have to take into account—and incorporate rather than hide—the *ecclesial* dimension of the theological work. The idea that Catholic academic theology can thrive or even survive independently from what happens in and to the church is an illusion.[9]

What Remains of the "Land O' Lakes Statement" (1967)

The identity crisis at the root of the situation of Catholic higher education is a bigger problem than the collapse of the credibility of the church, and it can't be blamed on church politics. Student enrollments are trending down, for a variety of reasons— from perceptions about academic competitiveness and future

---

[9] Sarah Coakley notes about non-Catholic universities a phenomenon that is not unknown in Catholic campuses: "The ironic result is that Divinity School students in these leading institutions may now find themselves more encouraged in the cultivation of a disciplined practice of prayer and asceticism by the *philosophy* professors in the university rather than by their own Divinity School leaders. Is this a rational or defensible state of affairs? That is an interesting question for debate, on which there is so far an almost deafening silence." Sarah Coakley, "Shaping the Field: A Transatlantic Perspective," in *Fields of Faith: Theology and Religious Studies for the Twenty-First Century*, ed. David F. Ford, Ben Quash, and Janet Martin Soskice, 39–55 (Cambridge: Cambridge University Press, 2005), 53.

employability to economic conditions related to the pandemic or other factors. Many institutions are dealing with deficits and feeling pressure to cut staff, gut programs, or lower the bar for what constitutes the kind of budget problems that allow for tenured faculty layoffs (often in violation of the colleges' faculty handbooks).[10]

There is no surer way of killing off a subject than having no teachers who teach it, and this is what is happening to theology in many Catholic colleges and universities. In seeking to address the bottom line and budget challenges, many schools are putting their very Catholic identity at risk as they position and market themselves as part of the mainstream arena of higher education. At the same time some conservative Catholic institutions are doubling down on their Catholic identity in ways that are concerning. These schools have a strong natural affinity with certain kinds of Catholics, as well as a supportive institutional partner in the clerical establishment, whereas liberal-progressive Catholic higher education has no such core strengths, and that may in part be its own doing. By embracing deconstruction of the neo-Scholastic hegemony since Vatican II fully, it is now suspicious of *any* Catholic institutional thinking, forgetting that without the institutions, a level of academic life is impossible. Theologians' concept of institution applied to the church should not stop at a sociological, political, or juridical level, but also take into account the theological dimensions specific to the church and its foundations as a sign of the mystery of salvation.[11]

---

[10] See Liam Adams, "Catholic Colleges Ignored Faculty Handbook Provisions in Layoffs, Report Alleges," *National Catholic Reporter*, June 7, 2021.

[11] See Giorgio Agamben, *The Kingdom and the Glory: For a Theological Genealogy of Economy and Government* (Stanford, CA: Stanford University Press, 2012; original Italian, Vicenza: Neri Pozza, 2007). Agamben's position as a *Querdenker* vis-à-vis theology is notable; so are his criticisms of the contemporary university system as it has evolved in a bureaucratized direction. See also his short article "Requiem for the Students," trans. D. Alan Dean, May 23, 2020, available online (Agamben here refers specifically to developments in Italy).

Our theology has been quite accommodating of the identity politics that have taken root since the 1960s, even if it is still perhaps too closely linked to a vision of Catholic higher education laid out more than fifty years ago in the "Land O' Lakes Statement," now showing its age. And, in a sort of culminating gesture, our theology adopted a view of 1990's *Ex Corde Ecclesiae* (and also the *Catechism of the Catholic Church* of 1992) based on the belief that John Paul II and the Vatican were imposing an unacceptably unilateral understanding of Catholicism and Catholic education.

Which is why locutions such as "in the Catholic tradition" or "in the Catholic heritage" entered the mission-statement language of so many Catholic universities in the last few years. "Hiring for mission" thus replaced "hiring Catholic," and met with mixed results. If "hiring Catholics does not in itself guarantee that the Catholic mission of these universities will be preserved and nurtured," as Peter Steinfels wrote back in 2007, the same can also be said also for hiring for mission.[12] One of the problems of hiring for mission is that the fear of ecclesiastical tyranny is still stronger than the fear of being put completely in the hands of technocrats. Theologians must deal with the fact that our culture and education systems—as well as religion—are part of a larger transition "from the disciplinary to the neoliberal regime, or the development from industrial capitalism to surveillance capitalism. . . . The neoliberal regime is not repressive."[13] Catholic theological anti-institutionalism, even though radical in its roots, has been welcomed by and functional to the neo-liberal system in our universities as well as in our societies.

Even as the capitalist culture of today's university model centralizes the business school, outsourcing its moral respectability to business-ethics programs, the liberal-progressive Catholic

---

[12] See Peter Steinfels, "Hiring Catholic—Hiring for Mission?" *Commonweal*, September 25, 2007.

[13] Han, *Vita Contemplativa*, 75, 77.

institutions are also making Catholic identity a matter of marketing and public relations. Since there is no constitutionally established church in the United States (as in Germany, for example), the Catholic educational and cultural structure still relies on an essentially ecclesial institutional system that benefits only marginally from the support of public institutions.[14]

We know about the Catholic conservatives' rejection of Pope Francis. But there is a liberal inability to understand the shift occurring at the magisterial level in the Catholic Church, where the discourse is moving away from "pelvic issues" to the crises brought on by globalization and corporatization. This shift has only tangentially affected Catholic theological academia in the Western hemisphere. Discussions on confronting racism, exclusion, and sexual violence are squarely within the mission of a Catholic university. But much less attention is devoted to the corporatization of the Catholic university and the way that administrators and faculty members alike have embraced it. Gerald Beyer, in *Just Universities*, writes that "like their secular counterparts, Catholic universities vary in the degree in which they have succumbed to corporatization and market fundamentalism."[15] Beyer makes the argument, following Henry Giroux's critique of "gated intellectuals," that not only those who work at a Catholic college or university, but all Catholics, need to be concerned with these issues, not simply their own agendas.

Something else to consider, to appreciate the difference from the times of the "Land O' Lakes Statement" in outlining a vision for higher Catholic education, is how the Catholic Church and

---

[14] For perspectives from the German-speaking world, see *Zur Zukunft der Theologie in Kirche, Universität und Gesellschaft*, ed. Gerhard Krieger (Quaestiones Disputatae, 283) (Freiburg: Herder, 2017).

[15] See Gerald J. Beyer, *Just Universities: Catholic Social Teaching Confronts Corporatized Higher Education* (New York: Fordham University Press, 2021). See also James F. Keenan, *University Ethics: How Colleges Can Build and Benefit from a Culture of Ethics* (Rowman & Littlefield, 2015).

the Catholic education system haven't been spared in this global age of resentment, grievance, and anger.[16] The resentment toward the ecclesiastical system has resulted from the fallout of the sex-abuse crisis, the refusal to deal with racism, and the apparent detachment from reality by members of the hierarchy. But there is also an anger toward the ecclesial vocation of Catholic institutions of education, in their alignment with the church, which has been identified not just historically but *essentially* with racism, colonialism, and sexism. It is a view that sees tradition as wholly oppressive rather than having the potential to possibly be liberating, as life denying rather than holding potential to be life affirming, and therefore viewed as not worth adhering to, much less saving. In an astonishing reversal of the ancient *extra ecclesiam, nulla salus* (no salvation outside the church), this attitude can be summed up as *extra ecclesiam, sola salus* (the only salvation is in leaving the church).

It is difficult to counter such an attitude—when justified anger with some aspects of the Catholic tradition turns into utter contempt. Among the questions we need to ask is how we save the Catholic tradition from the efforts of those who try to conscript it in the "culture wars" or to present it as intrinsically radical, conservative, liberal, or oppressive. An ecclesially interested theology is hemmed in by the broader political polarization in the United States, caught between the Scylla of neo-conservative Catholic studies and the Charybdis of Big Business, post-religious versions of DEI (diversity, equity, and inclusion).

What Remains of Departments of Theology and Religious Studies

Resentment and anger toward the institutional church present serious problems regarding the question of the mission of

---

[16] See Pankaj Mishra, *The Age of Anger: A History of the Present* (New York: Farrar, Straus, and Giroux, 2017).

academics, especially for theologians, in the context of a larger uncertainty of the mission of theology in Catholic higher education. If it is obvious that Catholic colleges and universities should not be engaged in proselytism, what's more controversial is the issue of the evangelizing and kerygmatic mission of these schools. What are departments of theology and/or religious studies in Catholic universities and colleges *for?* How did their roles change compared to the rise of other Catholic-mission-related entities on Catholic campuses (office for mission, campus ministry, centers and think tanks, and so on) and related to the creation of more intentional, faith-based academic departments, such as Catholic Studies, for example?[17] Do departments of theology and/or religious studies have a future on Catholic campuses?

Regarding the relationship between theology and religious studies in Catholic colleges and universities, one of the key questions is whether Catholic higher education can keep, as Sarah Coakley put it in the early 2000s, "the remainingly creative dimensions of the Enlightenment contrast between the 'study of religion' and 'Christian theology.'"[18] Now in the departments of theology and religious studies in Catholic universities it is more a problem of what *theologians* want to do than what religious-studies scholars usually do. This is an issue that speaks directly

---

[17] For a critical view, see Michael J. Byron, "Catholic Universities Must Teach Faith across Disciplines," *America*, February 8, 2016. *Contra*, see David P. Deavel, "The Collegiate Ideal Renewed: Catholic Studies as Newmanian Project," *A Word in Season* (Fall 2020), 57–74. As James Heft puts it bluntly and succinctly: "Catholic studies is here to stay. . . . On the other hand, the existence of CSPs is a tacit admission on the part of some administrators in faculty that their university no longer communicates a sufficiently integrated vision of Catholicism." James L. Heft, *The Future of Catholic Higher Education: The Open Circle* (New York: Oxford University Press, 2021), 229.

[18] Coakley, "Shaping the Field: A Transatlantic Perspective," 41, see also esp. 44–49. On the distinction between theology and religious studies, see also Francis Schüssler Fiorenza, "Theology in the University," *The Council of Societies for the Study of Religion Bulletin* 22 (April 1993): 34–39; and 23 (February 1994): 6–10.

to the local institutional context of many Catholic theologians. It concerns questions around what kind of Catholic identity there should be within the university, what the mission of these departments should be in light of their "competition" with other departments or units claiming the Catholic identity on campus, as well as questions concerning their relationship with the local church, the risks of confessionalism, the relationship between the normative and the descriptive in the teaching of theology and religious studies.

Leaving this issue of mission unresolved makes it easier to imagine a future without these departments on Catholic campuses. Substitutes already exist: institutes, centers, endowed chairs in Catholic/Christian topics in other schools (law and business schools), Catholic programs conferring degrees without any requirement of participation by the theology and/or religious-studies departments on those same campuses.

This "divide and conquer" strategy in distributing "the Catholic mission" in separate units in Catholic colleges has exposed theologians in departments of theology to the risk of becoming echo chambers dealing with their intra-Catholic fights. At the same time, more strategic Catholic faculty members in other fields and departments have captured the attention of students who have a personal and genuine interest in religion but avoid the anti-devotional *animus* of academic theology. These students, then, take theology courses from departments other than theology bringing personal investment to non-required courses, courses they choose intentionally, while theology departments argue mission and politically juggle their role: "There is an intense coyness about doctrinal or credal tradition, lest—it seems—the wider university look unfavourably on such commitment as offensive proselytism."[19]

---

[19] Coakley, "Shaping the Field: A Transatlantic Perspective," 48.

Once, it was assumed that Catholic colleges and universities must teach faith across disciplines. Now, even though the faith perspective on mainstream Catholic campuses tends to be articulated, thanks to Vatican II, in ecumenical, interreligious, inclusive, and non-proselytizing terms, that faith perspective has become controversial as a driver of overall educational mission.

Doing theology *in, with,* and *for* the church, as well as for the broader world, has become controversial not only for non-theological faculty, but sometimes also for theology and religious-studies departments on Catholic campuses. In addition to compatibility problems with *Ex Corde Ecclesiae*, this also presents compatibility problems with Pope Francis. If the perspective of lived faith is discarded from the outset, if the missionary and evangelizing dimension is discarded, one wonders what the progressives' Catholic enthusiasm for Francis is about.

Many progressive Catholics ignore conservative, traditional ways of being Catholic or even hold them in contempt. But we can't afford to ignore this shrinking window of opportunity for exercising the energy needed to give new life to a Catholic understanding of education. From *Laudato Si'* to *Fratelli Tutti* to *Laudate Deum,* Pope Francis is leading a movement that rejects Catholic exclusivism and neo-fundamentalism, that critiques neo-liberal capitalism, that seeks development of doctrine on the death penalty and the dismantling of a moral rigorism in the service of a bourgeois and conventional Catholicism. These teaching fit perfectly well with efforts emphasizing diversity and inclusion in a Catholic identity that goes beyond what the canon of Western civilization contains. Yet at the same time, the relief brought about by Pope Francis's disavowal of the culture-war agenda can sometimes work almost as a new kind of functional anti-Catholicism, in which Catholicism and Catholic culture are taken seriously only insofar as they support the technocratic paradigm of the contemporary university or one side of the two-party ideological agenda.

Often, those who ideologically embrace the social justice tradition of Catholicism are not interested in keeping courses in systematic theology, because they are not aware that theology is the essential language or dialect of the action of the church, embedded in the historical drama of the fight for the dignity of the human person, of the protection of the poor or vulnerable, and of the care of creation. Catholics today tend to favor the embodied testimony of the social prophets, but if we liquidate those who give words to experience and action, over time these prophetic actions do not transform into culture but dissolve.

In one of his latest books published in English, *The Unnamable Present*, Italian author Roberto Calasso (1941–2021) used opposing images of "terrorists and tourists" and "fundamentalism and Silicon Valley" to describe the divide of faith in contemporary society.[20] To presuppose a detachment from one's faith perspective as a prerequisite for scholarly objectivity and a condition for being at a university open to cultural and religious diversity would make us spiritual tourists who merely visit and choose to conceal or not to inhabit one religious tradition. This detachment also means that if faculty, students, and administrators decide that inhabiting our religious tradition is incompatible with contemporary academia, we are only legitimizing another religious canon while forsaking our own.[21]

While practices of discipleship precede reflection, reflection is essential for understanding the roots and the implications of praxis. They necessarily inform each other. The insistence on social justice, diversity, and inclusion—as commendable as it is—requires theological and doctrinal foundations, where

---

[20] Roberto Calasso, *The Unnamable Present*, trans. Richard Dixon (New York: Farrar Straus and Giroux, 2019).

[21] For discussion of the proliferation of "thin" bureaucratic rules that imperil and drive out "thick" ones, creating an implicit and shared canon, see Lorraine Daston, *Rules: A Short History of What We Live By* (Princeton, NJ: Princeton University Press, 2022).

the dimension of normativity is also considered—not rejected a priori. The intertwining of praxis and theology for Catholic institutions of higher learning needs to be articulated as elements of the mission and identity of the university or college. Catholic social thought can only be robustly understood and practiced on the basis of theological foundations—a theology that is differentiated from the apologetics of the tradition or of the papal magisterium. Surrendering Catholic education to a post-theological and post-ecclesial mode will sooner or later make social Catholicism not just politically and culturally irrelevant, but intellectually impossible to unpack and justify.

Catholic colleges and universities in the United States aren't alone in this. Other countries face similar challenges. In Germany, for example, theology departments in state universities are in conversation with the bishops and the seminaries over the direction and the future of Catholic theology. These kinds of discussions in Germany take a different shape than in the United States, in part because of the private-market nature of Catholic higher education in the United States, and in part because of the manifest estrangement from the institutional church. In the United States the term *institutional church* does not mean the bishops and the Vatican, but rather the importance of institutions as social structures that are embodied in concrete communities, apostolic works, parishes, programs, *as well as* ordained and in-stituted ministries, offices, bishops, popes, and the Vatican. These "institutions" exist within a broader conciliar, theological vision of the church as the whole people of God, a structured com-munion of missionary disciples.

It is important to be responsive to the threat that different forms of ecclesiastical despotism present to Catholic intellectual life. But it would be an illusion to think that Catholicism can survive, much less thrive, if we disregard the fate of Catholic academic institutions and the place of theology within them. To paraphrase Fr. Theodore Hesburgh, the university is one of the places where the church does its thinking. To lose the "Catholic" university would mean being left with a non-thinking, merely reactionary church.

This intra-Catholic war of attrition has led to an institutional and functional dissociation between theology and the church. Catholic theology has become increasingly absent from the radar of Catholic clerical and lay leaders (bishops, public intellectuals, and Catholic philanthropy that supports the cultural institutions of North American Catholicism). The monumentalized and memorialized "theology of Vatican II" often presents as anesthetic— an inability to read the "signs of the times." The freedom the theology academy gained at and after Vatican II had a cost: losing contact with the life of the church. In that space, traditionalist-oriented projects, more suited to the "culture wars" embraced by the bishops appointed by John Paul II and Benedict XVI, moved in, producing religious vocations to ordained ministry as well as intellectual vocations—in ways that have eluded progressive Catholic theology.

Part of this asymmetry between the two different theological and ecclesial projects was an anti-intellectualism. Catholic neo-conservatism and neo-traditionalism have been more able or willing to capitalize on the disappearance of the opposition between the expert *savants* on one side and the self-taught *autodidactes*—an opposition that was constitutive of the creation of the modern universities.

It turns out that in the world of the post-secular and *la revanche de Dieu*,[22] there is also *la revanche des autodidactes*, the resurgence of the self-taught, in regard to theology. Not only is this

---

[22] See Gilles Kepel, *La Revanche de Dieu: Chrétiens, juifs et musulmans à la reconquête du monde* (Paris: Seuil, 1991). Published in English as *The Revenge of God: The Resurgence of Islam, Christianity and Judaism in the Modern World* (University Park: Pennsylvania State University Press, 1994).

borne out in Catholicism, but in other Christian and religious traditions as well.[23]

What Remains of Vatican II Today

Pope Francis opened a new phase in the reception of Vatican II in ways that do not quite fit the usual theological-political alignments of liberal vs. conservatives. On January 11, 2021, in the "Letter of the Holy Father Francis to the Prefect of the Congregation for the Doctrine of the Faith on Access of Women to the Ministries of Lector and Acolyte," the pope described his decision in terms of the "horizon of renewal outlined by the Second Vatican Council" and "in line with the Second Vatican Council." Later that month, on January 30, 2021, the pope made pointed remarks in "Address of His Holiness Pope Francis to Participants in the Meeting Promoted by the National Catechetical Office of the Italian Episcopal Conference":

> The Council is the magisterium of the Church. Either you are with the Church and therefore you follow the Council, and if you do not follow the Council or you interpret it in your own way, as you wish, you are not with the Church. We must be demanding and strict on this point. The Council should not be negotiated in order to have more of these. . . . No, the Council is as it is. And this problem that we are experiencing, of selectivity with respect to the Council, has been repeated throughout history with other Councils.

As with other teachings by Francis, these statements spoke in a particularly directed way to US Catholicism. During the

---

[23] See Olivier Roy, *La Sainte Ignorance: Le temps de la religion sans culture* (Paris: Seuil, 2008). Published in English as *Holy Ignorance: When Religion and Culture Part Ways* (New York: Columbia University Press, 2010).

tumultuous relationship between Francis and US traditionalist Catholics, some bishops and clerics have sought to advance a theologically defensible conservative interpretation of Vatican II, in order to counter the extremist views of former papal nuncio to the United States, Archbishop Carlo Maria Viganò, who in online postings has taken a position that is hard to distinguish from pure and simple rejection of the council's teachings.

A growing quasi-schismatic group of Catholics openly rejects the "Bergoglian" magisterium as they follow in the footsteps of Viganò. Against them and against Viganò, Bishop Robert Barron spoke about attacks on Vatican II as a "disturbing trend,"[24] and Thomas Weinandy, former executive director of the Secretariat for Doctrine and Pastoral Practices of the United States Conference of Catholic Bishops, chastised Viganò for challenging the council's authenticity. [25]

Between the magisterium and open rejection there's more than theological interpretation to consider. The alliance of conservative American Catholicism with MAGA Trumpism reflects another element, and also says something about the reception of Vatican II; the fascination some have for a quasi-Caesarean political leadership is a symptom of the council's crisis of reception.

Yet even if this is most evident among the extreme voices on the conservative side of the spectrum, it's not a uniquely conservative problem. There are broader systemic phenomena at play that in the last few years have brought about fault lines also within the liberal-progressive side.

The first is an "interruption" of serious examination of Vatican II in the scholarly tradition. Studying the council requires fluency in the languages of the documents in Latin and other

---

[24] Bishop Robert Barron, "Pope Francis and Vatican II," 2020 Napa Institute keynote address, August 15, 2020. Available on YouTube.

[25] See Thomas G. Weinandy, "A Response to Archbishop Viganò's Letter about Vatican II," *Catholic World Report*, August 13, 2020.

languages. It also requires an intellectual ecosystem in which theology is grounded in—and in conversation with—church history and the history of theology, not just social sciences.[26] An imbalance exists between the reluctance to engage the theology of Vatican II in its doctrinal and systematic aspects, on the one side, and the dedicated scholarship on the local/national histories of Vatican II, on the other side.[27]

A closely related issue to this schism is a breakdown of the coexistence and collaboration that used to characterize the working relationship among professional theologians, Catholic laity, and the institutional and hierarchical church. What we are seeing now is the result of dangerous intra-Catholic tensions—ecclesial and political—that have developed in this country over the years since the publication of multivolume commentaries on the documents of Vatican II.[28] There seems to be more space now in the Catholic theological academy for pre- and anti-Vatican II theology on one side, and a post–Vatican II theology with fewer discernible ecclesial commitments on the other side. The theology of Vatican II is itself caught in something of an intellectual and ecclesial no-man's land.

In the early 2000s, sexual and financial scandals brought about a moral and legal crisis, and also a theological one. And the crisis is deeper rooted than that revealed by the early disclosures of the

---

[26] For example, there is still no consensus on the English translation, the last one of which is now more than twenty-five years old (Austin Flannery, 1996); this was preceded by the one edited by Norman Tanner, SJ, in 1990, and that by Walter Abbott, SJ, in 1966. There are important studies on America and Vatican II. The last American history of Vatican II was published in 2008 during the pontificate of Benedict XVI: John O'Malley, *What Happened at Vatican II* (Cambridge, MA: Harvard University Press, 2008).

[27] See, for example, Joseph P. Chinnici, *American Catholicism Transformed: From the Cold War through the Council* (New York: Oxford University Press, 2021).

[28] The English translation of the three volumes edited by Herbert Vorgrimler in 1967–68; the three volumes edited by René Latourelle and published by Paulist Press in 1987; and the Rediscovering Vatican II Series published in the early 2000s by Paulist Press.

sex-abuse scandal. Anger at an institution viewed as unresponsive (at best) on key social issues led many to the idea that the church had lost all religious and moral authority and thus that Vatican II had as well; its authors and episcopal leaders, the generations of its interpreters since then, and an entire tradition of studies have been regarded as irrelevant. And the growing resentment and distrust is not just an anti-historical mentality. Rather, the distrust arises from the belief that Vatican II did not engage with issues of gender and race in as radical a way as the times demanded, and as readings of the gospel today demand.

The perception grew that the debates at Vatican II, as well as the post-conciliar historical and hermeneutical debate, were dominated by European white male clergy. Among the examples that have been highlighted in a list of deepening distrust are these: the theology of Vatican II still points to the problematic issue and ongoing work (albeit with some limitations) against anti-Semitism with the church itself. Vatican II works less effectively regarding the role of women in the church, and even less effectively regarding the issue of abuse—whether sexual abuse, the abuse of authority, or the abuse of power. Vatican II shows the shortcomings of an early 1960s theology—developed in an early, post-imperial Catholicism just beginning to understand the postcolonial world. Now the disruption of the global order has revealed the inadequacy of that theology, as well as of its bishop-centered ecclesiology.

There is also a global, ecumenical, and interreligious factor: the shift in perceptions of ecumenism and interreligious dialogue between the time of the council and our post-9/11, twenty-first-century world. We have moved from a narrative of encounter to a narrative of clash and conflict. The work of 1960s and 1970s Catholicism called for something different. Catholicism now has to engage with more assertive (both religiously and politically) faiths around the world, as well as with a more assertive secularism. This has coincided with a rise of converts who bring a different set of expectations to their understanding of church tradition, which gives greater emphasis to the fathers of the church, the catechism, and papal teaching than to the conciliar tradition included in Vatican II.

This in turn introduces new interpretations and questions regarding historical periods: Was Vatican II really the beginning of dialogue with secular culture and with other religions? Or did Vatican II simply miss the roots of radical, political Islam? Did Vatican II embrace decolonization? Or did it actually participate in extending the life of colonial theology?

Perceptions about the relevance or irrelevance of Vatican II vary from person to person and from place to place. In Latin America, for instance, Vatican II is still highly regarded both in the church and in academia, while in the United States opinion is more divided. Both views prove just how the global conversation on the council is affected; and how the tumultuous ecclesiological and cultural changes substantively and substantially influence the approach to Vatican II around the world.

What has happened since the early 2000s on both the institutional and intellectual levels raises questions over the historical role of Vatican II in the global church. Was it the beginning of a new Catholic history, or a parenthesis in the larger postwar parenthesis of the liberal order, which itself is now in crisis? A rhetoric that posits Vatican II as the beginning of the intellectual and moral crisis of Catholicism (nostalgia for the pre-conciliar period) is set against the rhetoric of Vatican II as the last gasp of catholicity (nostalgia for the conciliar era and the first period after the council). Francis's pontificate is showing how key a contribution the theology of Vatican II has been for the transition from a European-centered Catholicism to a global one. At the same time, this moment in the globalization of the church is also showing the limits of Vatican II.

Especially in the United States, opposition to Pope Francis finds its roots in opposition to Vatican II. It is also true that the problematic range of positions regarding Francis and Vatican II in the United States helps us understand how the council's documents may be able to serve the church today—and in that, perhaps suggests what can be done to improve the reception and application of those documents.

There appear to be limits to what Francis's faithful reception of Vatican II can accomplish. And given the ecclesial split over Francis's pontificate, it's hard to imagine the calling of another general council anytime soon. Still, there is reason to believe that Vatican II could find new life in local and national expressions of synodality, giving a jolt of energy to the ecclesial process while, at the same time, addressing some of the gaps left by the theology and the teachings of the council.

2

The University and the Interrupted Reception of Vatican II

Recognizing the Interruption and the Gap in the Reception of the Council

When we talk about Vatican II today, it is essential to acknowledge the vast gap between the "horizon of expectations" raised by the council and the situation of the Catholic Church today.[1] Vatican II called Catholics to unity: unity in the one human family, with non-Christians and nonbelievers, with Christians of other traditions, and with fellow Catholics. But in these last few years we have seen that the fundamental call of Vatican II to unity through *reconciliation* often turned into a source of bitter division and contention, at times in a dangerous flirtation with schism. This is paradoxical because reconciliation is maybe even more of an original concept coming from an intuitive call for church reform. The division around Vatican II—and in the last

---

[1] See Reinhart Koselleck, *Futures Past: On the Semantics of Historical Time* (New York: Columbia University Press, 2004). For original German, see *Vergangene Zukunft: Zur Semantik geschichtlicher Zeiten* (Frankfurt am Main: Suhrkamp, 1979), esp. 255–75.

few years on the Synod on Synodality[2]—is on full display, even though in disguise, in Catholic colleges and universities.

We have seen this decline of the authority of Vatican II in the church with shocking clarity in the opposition against the pontificate of Francis. This is more than a chronological overlap. There is a parallel between the rejection of Vatican II and the relationship between neo-conservative Catholicism and Pope Francis. The opposition to Pope Francis is rooted in the opposition to Vatican II—a theological crisis that did not begin with his pontificate.

The problem is ecclesial and theological, and it has profound consequences for the ways in which all Catholics experience their life of faith in the church. This crisis is also a crisis of academic culture within the church, bearing consequences the kind of education we provide in Catholic schools (not only colleges and universities), and it is tied to the history and memory of Vatican II.

Despite several limitations in the wording of the final documents related to the need of the church to reckon with the past and a tendency to look at history as *magistra vitae*, the teacher of life (an approach that the sex-abuse crisis and the post-colonial critical theory seriously put in question in recent times), Vatican II took history seriously.[3] John O'Malley noted that Vatican II was more historically conscious than any previous council, attempting to treat religious truth in its historical dimension with as much earnestness as had traditionally been applied to its metaphysical dimension.[4] To do the same thing for the history of the post–Vatican II period is to seek to identify different historical phases

---

[2] See Christoph Theobald, *Un nouveau concile qui ne dit pas son nom? Le synode sur la synodalité, voie de pacification et de créativité* (Paris: Salvator, 2023).

[3] See Massimo Faggioli, "Que reste-t-il de Vatican II? Sexisme, racisme, crise des abus et régimes d'historicité dans l'Église," *Revue Théologique de Louvain* (2024).

[4] See John W. O'Malley, "Reform, Historical Consciousness, and Vatican II's *Aggiornamento*," in *Theological Studies* 32, no. 4 (1971): 573–601; see also Ormond Rush, *The Vision of Vatican II: Its Fundamental Principles* (Collegeville, MN: Liturgical Press, 2019), esp. 165–87.

in order to comprehend the origins of a crisis in the reception of Vatican II.

The reception of a council—for instance, Trent or Vatican II— takes a long time. Some estimate it takes at least a century for full implementation. The greatest historian of the council of Trent, the German priest Hubert Jedin, remarked in the very first lines of his multi-volume *History of the Council of Trent*, that the first century after the end of the council was shaped by the clash of historical and theological narratives on the council between the Venetian Servite Brother Paolo Sarpi and the Roman Jesuit Francesco Sforza Pallavicino. Only three centuries later, in the middle of the twentieth century, did it become possible to write an account of the theological and ecclesial turning point that Trent was—with a record of something more than a battle between "accusation and defense."[5]

At the same time, choosing a mechanistic periodization—that is, the expectation that the full reception of Vatican II will *necessarily* happen within, say, the next fifty or one-hundred years—is risky because it ignores church history, in which there have been failed councils: councils that did not accomplish their stated goals (the Council of Ferrara-Florence of 1438–49, a council of "union" with the Eastern Orthodox Churches), councils that fundamentally missed a deep understanding of significant currents of culture or religion (the Fifth Lateran Council, 1512–17, concluded immediately before the beginning of the Reformation), or councils that were overwhelmed by external factors and whose trajectories became substantially different from what the councils originally imagined (the Council of Moscow for the Russian Orthodox Church, 1917–18).

---

[5] Hubert Jedin, *Geschichte des Konzils von Trient*, vol. 1 (Freiburg 1950), V ("Vorwort"): "Seit Sarpi und Pallavicino, also seit dreihundert Jahren, wartet die Welt auf eine Geschichte des Konzils von Trient, die mehr ist als Anklage und Verteidigung." I thank Mark Massa, SJ, for this important reminder.

Vatican II is not a failed council. Despite the well-known tensions and divergences between different hermeneutics, there is a fundamental consensus between papal magisterium, the *sensus fidelium* in the people of God, and the theological tradition on the teachings of Vatican II represent a development, a growth in our understanding (*Dei Verbum*, no. 8) of God's revelation. If anything, the signs of our times evidence the necessity of the reorientation of the Catholic Church to Vatican II.

But we live in a time of interruption to the reception of Vatican II. This interruption has been there for quite some time, and we need to understand the present state of the reception of Vatican II in order to avoid being trapped into narratives that posit a direction toward a predetermined end.

Phases in the Reception of Vatican II

In the literature on Vatican II scholars have identified different periodizations of the post-conciliar period.[6] Periodizations of the post–Vatican II years still tend to cling to perspectives tied to national or (at best) continental histories. Few of them have tried to deal with the fact that Vatican II was a council for the global church, received by the global church in a timeline that varies dramatically from country to country and continent to continent. We still do not have a global history of the post–Vatican II Catholic Church, and even less an accepted narrative of the global post–Vatican II period—something the longer timeline

---

[6] See Massimo Faggioli, *Vatican II: The Battle for Meaning* (Mahwah, NJ: Paulist Press, 2012). For the first twenty years after the council, see Hermann J. Pottmeyer, "A New Phase in the Reception of Vatican II: Twenty Years of Interpretation of the Council," in *The Reception of Vatican II*, ed. Giuseppe Alberigo, Jean-Pierre Jossua, and Joseph A. Komonchak (Washington, DC: Catholic University of America Press, 1987). At that time Pottmeyer identified a first phase of enthusiasm, followed by another phase of disappointment or reaction, and concluded with a phase of synthesis that brought more coherence to the interpretation of the council.

of reception to previous councils made possible, as their impact could be measured in a Catholic Church that was predominantly European and Mediterranean.

But it is possible to divide the first three decades after Vatican II into three periods. The first is the age of *Vatican II acknowledged, received, or rejected*—the fifteen years between 1965 and the end of the 1970s: the time of the implementation of the liturgical reform, of the translations and dissemination of the final texts of the council, of the great commentaries written mostly by those men who helped draft the final texts of the council. The rejection of Vatican II was limited to small fringes of extremists and traditionalists—fringes both in the church and society—who articulated their opposition based on a nostalgia for pre-secularization Christendom and allegations of Vatican II's violation of the continuity of the tradition. The opposition was not yet based on sociopolitical arguments, that is, the alleged evidence of the failure of Vatican II to reframe the relations between the church and the world.

The second period is *Vatican II remembered, reconsidered, and expanded*—the 1980s. It is the time of John Paul II's effort to stabilize the reception of Vatican II by keeping "letter and spirit" together (the Extraordinary Assembly of the Bishops' Synod of 1985) and to "institutionalize" Vatican II (the *Code of Canon Law* of 1983; the 1992 Catechism, a project launched after the 1985 Synod). At the same time John Paul II pushed the teaching of the church beyond the boundaries of the letter of Vatican II, especially on ecumenism and interreligious dialogue (in particular with regard to Judaism and Islam).

The third period is *Vatican II historicized and lamented*—the 1990s and the early 2000s. This is the period of the effort to write the master narrative on the history of Vatican II,[7] while

---

[7] See *History of Vatican II*, 5 vols., ed. Giuseppe Alberigo. English edition ed. Joseph A. Komonchak (Maryknoll, NY: Orbis Books, 1995–2006).

at the same time attempting to narrow down the import of the openings of the council by the institutional church in a rebuke to the appeals to the "spirit." But still among Catholics, across the aisles of division, there was a fidelity (if sometimes nominalistic) to the letter of Vatican II and to the legitimacy of the conciliar tradition that extends to and includes Vatican II.

There is also the possibility of a different periodization that is relevant to understanding the interrupted reception of Vatican II. For a long time the 1960s have been seen as a decisive decade in terms of Christianity's encounter with secular and pluralistic modernity. But in terms of secular modernity's impact on relations among different Christian traditions, it was the 1990s—with the explosion of the culture wars—that was crucial.[8] In this third period, thirty years from the celebration of the council, the interruption of the reception of Vatican II began, activating the diversion of large donors (in particular in US Catholicism) away from an *ecclesial* reception of Vatican II.

On the one side, a key factor in the interruption of the reception of Vatican II is the beginning, in academic theology, of symptoms of detachment from the institutional church, but also from a connection with the lived experience of the people of God, in ways that are more drastic than anywhere else in global Catholicism. It is the rise of a post-ecclesial horizon thanks to a stark polarity between institution and society.[9] Not just a healthy relativization of the institutional church in favor of the transcendent, it was the failure to recognize that the institutional element in Catholicism *also* allows for different kinds of theological-

---

[8] James Davison Hunter popularized the term *culture wars* in his book *Culture Wars: The Struggle to Define America* (New York: Basic Books, 1991) describing tensions between religious and secular trends as well as alternative visions of the role of the family in society. See also Christopher Caldwell, "The Fateful Nineties," *First Things* (October 2023).

[9] About this, see the books by Italian political philosopher Roberto Esposito, the most recent of which is *Instituting Thought: Three Paradigms of Political Ontology*, trans. Mark Epstein (Cambridge, UK: Polity, 2021).

spiritual cultures and different members to build the catholicity of the church.

On the other side, there is the neo-conservative ideologization of Catholicism, still present in the 1990s with a certain amount of respect (at least nominally) for Vatican II.[10] It is the long wave and the American Catholic version of the "comeback of God" in global politics.[11] But there is also the dangerous turn on its head of a clerical culture of identification of catholicity with one particular model of papal leadership. On the conservative and traditionalist side of the spectrum, in the early 2000s the papacy of John Paul II was still also providing a mantle of legitimacy for the respectability of Vatican II among neo-conservative circles.

Benedict XVI's interpretation of Vatican II was different from John Paul II's. From Benedict's famous—and often misquoted— speech to the Roman Curia of December 22, 2005, onward, the polarity of "continuity and reform *versus* discontinuity and rupture" became a kind of simplistic mantra. The argument of "continuity with the tradition of the council," presented at the beginning as an argument against the Lefebvrite thesis of Vatican II as a "rupture" with the Catholic tradition, soon turned against any idea of "reform"—which was in fact an integral part of that pivotal speech by Benedict XVI.[12]

The protection given by the papacy to the legitimacy of Vatican II lasted only until Benedict's pontificate and made it dangerously easier to trade one kind of ecclesial source of identity for another in favor of a new papalism. This happened at the expense

[10] See Massimo Borghesi, *Catholic Discordance: Neoconservatism vs. the Field Hospital Church of Pope Francis*, trans. Barry Hudock (Collegeville, MN: Liturgical Press, 2021).

[11] See Gilles Kepel, *The Revenge of God: The Resurgence of Islam, Christianity and Judaism in the Modern World* (University Park: Pennsylvania State Press, 1994). Original French: *La revanche de Dieu* (Paris: Seuil, 1991). Translated in several languages.

[12] See Joseph A. Komonchak, "Novelty in Continuity: Pope Benedict's interpretation of Vatican II," *America*, February 2, 2009.

of a healthy sense of the Catholic tradition—ironic or tragic for a theologian like Joseph Ratzinger, who was among the main authors and interpreters of key documents of the council such as *Lumen Gentium* and *Dei Verbum*.

One of the effects of the identification in the United States between Benedict XVI's pontificate and Catholic resistance to theological progressivism was the creation of the premises for the transition from Vatican II conservatism to a neo-traditionalist rejection of Vatican II among the Catholic intellectual and clerical elites. It was a key turning point, a rejection not just of vague appeals to the "spirit" of the documents of Vatican II, but also to the letter of the documents and their theology. The explosive effects of this expansion of the anti-conciliar Catholic front became clear beginning in March 2013 with the election of Pope Francis.

A New Phase with Francis

The interruption in the reception of Vatican II has escalated during the pontificate of Francis, and a reactionary move-ment—also from inside the church—opened the possibility of a long-term crisis of ecclesial communion. This started even before the beginning of his pontificate; neo-conservative and neo-traditionalist voices among bishops, theologians, and politi-cians in the United States suddenly felt orphaned on February 11, 2013, when Benedict XVI announced his resignation. This sense of loss was particularly acute in the United States because of the (largely mistaken) sentiment that Joseph Ratzinger/ Benedict XVI definitively turned the table on Vatican II, settling forever the disputation on the interpretation of the council—first as cardinal prefect of the Vatican Congregation for the Doctrine of the Faith, and later as pope.

But the globalization and de-Occidentalizing of Catholi-cism—presciently intuited by Vatican II—affected the conclave of 2013. This was not just a pope "almost from the end of the world," as Francis remarked in his first address to the people gathered in St. Peter's that night of March 2013. Francis's pontificate coincided with, and in part contributed to, the transformation of the transatlantic ecclesial bond between the papacy and American Catholicism.[13] From the very first weeks and months of his pontificate, Francis showed a full and unequivocal receptivity to Vatican II, thanks in part to theological and ecclesial debate on Vatican II, which over the past sixty years has never ceased to be part of the life of the universal church.

Pope Francis inaugurated a new phase in the reception of Vatican II, not only with the disappearance of the defense of traditionalist, anti–Vatican II issues from the agenda of Pope Francis and his Roman Curia, but due to a novel change. The pontificates of the last century all were defined (to various differing degrees) by the historical-theological debate in relation to the council: Pius XII, the pope most cited in the documents of Vatican II, and his decision not to re-convene Vatican I; John XXIII, convener of the council; Paul VI, who was explicitly elected to continue the council, leading him to its conclusion at the cost of significant compromises with some of the dreams of reform emerging from the council; John Paul I, the "second row" council father; John Paul II, the last pope to be a member of Vatican II, where he was a key figure and "stabilizer" of the council simultaneously; Benedict XVI, one of the most important periti of Vatican II, and as pope and cardinal the most important theological "enforcer" of the council and its interpretations.

Pope Francis ended this line of popes involved in Vatican II, as he was ordained in 1969, but also due to his heritage and work with the church in Latin America. The Argentine Jesuit Jorge Mario Bergoglio perceived Vatican II as a matter that should not

---

[13] See Massimo Faggioli and Bryan Froehle, *Global Catholicism: Between Disruption and Encounter,* Studies in Global Catholicism, 1 (Leiden: Brill, 2024).

be reinterpreted or restricted, but implemented and (depending on the issue) expanded.[14] His reluctance to theorize on different hermeneutics of Vatican II was neither indifference to, nor ignorance of, the centrality of the hermeneutical question.

Faithful to the intuitions of Vatican II also as an event (expressed only in a partial manner in the final documents of the council), Pope Francis speaks of the theological value of spiritual poverty as a condition of accepting the gospel of Jesus Christ and proposes a radical and continuous need for the church and Christians to align themselves with the poor, in both existential and economic poverty. This emphasis on social justice is part of Francis's ecclesiology—an "ecclesiology of the people of God"—that has clear implications for a more conciliar style and synodal structure of church government.[15] This can be seen in Francis's documents and gestures of dialogue with Islam, parallel only with John Paul II's documents and gestures toward dialogue with the Jews.

Yet the problem of the authority of Vatican II as part of the tradition has still not been resolved, and it has become a more serious and pressing question in the situation Pope Francis inherited. With Francis there is a particular way of talking about Vatican II without explicitly mentioning it or quoting Vatican II documents. This is also an expressed refusal to refer to Vatican II and its documents in a legalistic way. Francis talks about Vatican II without falling into veterans' sentimentality. He does this through the Catholic tradition of which Vatican II has become a part: through quotations of Paul VI, by allowing documents of bishops' conferences to speak in his encyclicals and exhortations,

---

[14] See Massimo Faggioli, *Pope Francis: Tradition in Transition* (Mahwah, NJ: Paulist Press, 2015), and *The Liminal Papacy of Pope Francis: Moving toward Global Catholicity* (Maryknoll, NY: Orbis Books, 2020).

[15] On synodality especially see *For a Missionary Reform of the Church: The Civiltà Cattolica Seminar*, ed. Antonio Spadaro and Carlos Maria Galli, foreword by Massimo Faggioli (Mahwah, NJ: Paulist Press, 2017).

and by recovering the fundamental intuitions of Vatican II as an integral part of the mission of the church.

Francis's philosophy of holding the polarity in tension[16] is part of his continuing work to resolve polarization between extremes on Vatican II: between those who see Vatican II as too modern to be Catholic, and those who see it as too Catholic to be modern; between the institutional status quo narrative, and a post-ecclesial narrative; between the spirit and the letter; between *ressourcement* and *aggiornamento*; between defense of a Tridentine clerical system, and naive dreams of a *tabula rasa*.

One of most important contributions of Francis to the reception of Vatican II has probably been related to revealing the non-ecclesial or anti-ecclesial spirits that drive the rejection of Vatican II. We have seen this with some reactions to the *motu proprio* of July 16, 2021, *Traditionis Custodes,* on the issue of the liturgical reform, which is historically how those in opposition to the teachings of Vatican II tried to find an impossible legitimacy using an argument from tradition—whereas the argument is actually a rejection of the dynamic way Catholic tradition works.

The Current Ecclesial Disruption and Vatican II

The opposition we've seen against the pontificate of Francis in the church defies imagination as well as distorts our expectations about the church. We have witnessed unprecedented, rebellious challenges—sometimes coming from members of the clergy—to the legitimacy of the bishop of Rome that are clearly incompatible with the *sensus ecclesiae.* It is a phenomenon not limited to social media sound bites. It is fundamentally different from other

---

[16] See Massimo Borghesi, *The Mind of Pope Francis: Jorge Mario Bergoglio's Intellectual Journey*, trans. Barry Hudock (Collegeville, MN: Liturgical Press, 2018).

kinds of "dissent" against some aspects of papal teaching we've seen under Paul VI, John Paul II, and Benedict XVI.

We cannot ignore the context in which this ecclesial disruption occurs. First, there has been a change in the perception of Vatican II from the early post-conciliar period. Previously, Vatican II was considered among the most important events in church history. Some saw it as a deliverance, others as a catastrophe, but all agreed that it changed the church. For over fifty years, this verdict stood more or less unchallenged. No longer. Postmodern critics deconstructed the grand historical "metanarratives" in which the revolutions could have a central place. The rise of a global, postcolonial or de-colonial sensibility has called into question Vatican II's seemingly most significant achievements, but more fundamentally, the "regime of historicity" in which the era of Vatican II was understood and now needs to be reconsidered.[17]

Vatican II has also fallen victim to Catholic theological discourse in the university, in an incoherent mix of "memory and forgetting" that is part of our "presentist" understanding of history, in which identity is the driving force.[18] And within the university as well, digitalization and information have affected the church's sense of the past and the tradition: "Time increasingly disintegrates and becomes a mere succession of point-like presences. . . . There is no narrative to give it structure. . . . Temporal architectures erode."[19]

---

[17] See François Hartog, *Regimes of Historicity* (New York: Columbia University Press, 2015); in French, *Régimes d'historicité: Présentisme et expériences du temps* (Paris: Seuil, 2003). Also idem, *Chronos: L'Occident aux prises avec le temps* (Paris: Gallimard, 2020).

[18] "Awareness of being embedded in secular, serial time, with all its implications of continuity, yet of 'forgetting' the experience of this continuity—product of the ruptures of the late eighteenth century—engenders the need for a narrative of 'identity.'" Benedict R. O'G. Anderson, *Imagined Communities: Reflections on the Origin and Spread of Nationalism* (London: Verso, 2006 [1983]), 205.

[19] Byung-Chul Han, *Vita Contemplativa: In Praise of Inactivity* (Medford, MA: Polity, 2024), 49.

The Christian and Catholic tradition in the West has become one of the targets of what Indian essayist Pankaj Mishra calls "the age of anger"—a world in which people are unable to enjoy the promises of freedom, stability, and prosperity and are increasingly susceptible to demagogues—a sea change that also is seen within the Catholic Church.[20] The context for the ecclesial disruption has been varied across the globe, but in the United States the situation shows in a very particular way: while the narrative of the Catholic left about Vatican II isn't completely agreed on, on the right side of the spectrum the view of Vatican II as a catastrophe has resisted the postmodernist deconstruction, for different reasons. In just twenty years this is a church whose members have seen the pendulum swing from the Great Jubilee of 2000 to the revelation of sexual abuse involving some of the most powerful members of the hierarchy, where US Catholicism has been "ground zero" for the global abuse crisis in the church. Theological and political polarization have fueled one another and become a theologization of political identities and a politicization of the ecclesial discourse.

Another key factor is the shift in perceptions regarding ecumenism and interreligious dialogue between the time of the council and this post-9/11, new Cold War, twenty-first-century world. We have moved from a narrative of dialogue and encounter to a narrative of clash and conflict. Unlike the 1960s and 1970s, Catholicism now has to engage with the growth and growing assertiveness (both religiously and politically) of faiths around the world, as well as with the rise and assertiveness of secularism mixed with post-Enlightenment thinking. This has coincided for

---

[20] Pankaj Mishra, *Age of Anger: A History of the Present from Rousseau to ISIS* (New York: Farrar, Straus, and Giroux, 2017), 327. Mishra called Pope Francis "the most convincing and influential public intellectual today. . . . In a piquant irony, he is the moral voice of the church that was the main adversary of Enlightenment intellectuals as they built the philosophical scaffolding of a universal commercial society."

Catholicism with a rise of converts who bring a different set of expectations to their understanding of church tradition, which gives greater emphasis to the fathers of the church, the catechism, and papal teaching than to the conciliar tradition, including Vatican II. And this in turn introduces new interpretations of historical periods. Overall, the enormous gap is undeniable in terms of expectations between the generation of Catholics that grew up with Vatican II and the new generations in our parishes, classrooms, and workplaces. The situation of the church and the world of today echoes fewer of the the "joys and hopes" and more of "the griefs and the anxieties" (*luctus et angor*), in the words immediately following the incipit of *Gaudium et Spes*.

But there are also systematic theological weaknesses in the reception and transmission of the conciliar teaching that have made Catholicism an engine of anger and disenchantment for some, and a refuge from the storm of the crisis of the secular liberal order for others, including:

- the liturgical debate as part of postmodern identity politics and the "culture wars";
- ecclesiology reduced to mimic social imagination (from what Robert Bellarmine described as *societas perfecta* to secular models of a "perfect society"), and an ecclesial imagination largely surprised if not puzzled by Francis's call to synodality—the synodal "walking together" having to fight against a "walking out" mentality according to the new *extra ecclesiam, sola salus* (where the only salvation is in leaving the church);
- a loss of the theology of *Dei Verbum* on the approach to God's revelation as sacramental, open to growth in understanding, fundamentally different from both intellectualism and doctrinalism;
- the reduction of religion to ideas and to ethics, in an environment dominated by the sometimes-utopian nature of

prophetic indictment for the voice of religion in our public discourse;[21]

- the embrace of economic and social libertarianism (such as we've seen during the COVID-19 pandemic) contributing to the crisis of our democracy—a result of the *damnatio memoriae*, the result of the intentional disregard of *Gaudium et Spes* (among the most important documents of Vatican II for Pope Francis);

- a reduction of the conciliar doctrine on religious liberty to the "liberty of the Church" (*libertas ecclesiae*) echoing medieval Christendom;

- a politically partisan version of interfaith and interconfessional dialogue that has made urgent the need for intra-Catholic ecumenism;

- the globalization of the American "culture wars" that has given us the grim dividend of a visible lack of unity on critical domestic issues in light of the January 6, 2021, violent assault on Capitol Hill and related to international emergencies (such as the war in Ukraine and between Israel and Hamas): a lack of unity does not just have to do with policies, but is related to the moral and spiritual nature of the clash between democracy and authoritarianism.

The way in which conciliar teachings have been disregarded go on. But the most disturbing phenomenon is the transition from a crisis of ecclesial authority to a crisis of the authority of Vatican II and therefore a collapsing of a healthy sense of the tradition: of a dynamic and organic idea of the tradition; of the letter of the tradition not as a paradigm of understanding, but as an expression of the act of understanding; of a shift from cognitive

---

[21] See M. Cathleen Kaveny, *Prophecy without Contempt: Religious Discourse in the Public Square* (Cambridge, MA: Harvard University Press, 2018), 245–46.

and propositional to a personalist and dialogical understanding of revelation.[22]

The public debate in the church among theologians and bishops seems to have been replaced by a creeping schism created by the ones who see in the interpretation of Vatican II a point of rupture more symbolic than textual. From this standpoint we are now well beyond the dialectic "letter vs. spirit" or "event vs. documents." No longer just the spirit or the event, but also the same letter and the documents of Vatican II are now under the influence of revisionism and revanchism. The texts of Vatican II too are subject to growth in understanding. But the current debate is more about religious ideologies than about the conciliar texts.

For a country rich in technological, material, academic, and intellectual resources like the United States, the most common and tragic aspect of the crisis of reception of Vatican II is the "interruption" in the scholarly tradition of studying the council. This is far from a purely theoretical problem: in a recent article, Australian Jesuit Gerald O'Collins pointed out that the English translations of the documents of Vatican II basically *deleted* explicit references to *lectio divina*, mistranslating the term as "spiritual reading," which does not include the aspect of meditation and which can include engagement with non-scriptural texts.[23]

Related to this kind of diminishment is the breakdown we see of the coexistence and collaboration that used to characterize the "working relationship" among professional theologians, Catholic laity, and the institutional and hierarchical church. For the church in Latin America and in Europe, for example, one can clearly see

---

[22] See the commentary on *Dei Verbum* by Joseph Ratzinger, "Dogmatic Constitution on Divine Revelation," in *Commentary on the Documents of Vatican II*, ed. Herbert Vorgrimler, vol. 3 (New York: Herder and Herder, 1969), 155–98.

[23] See Gerald O'Collins, "Retrieving Lectio Divina at Vatican II and After," in *The Way* [journal of UK Jesuits], 60/4 (October 2021), 87–100, esp. 93–94.

that in the post–Vatican II period there have been three distinct phases: 1) the honeymoon between bishops and theologians at Vatican II; 2) a time of divorce or separation beginning in the late 1970s and 1980s until the early 2000s; 3) glimpses of reconciliation, due to the pontificate of Francis in this last decade. But this reconciliation among professional theologians, Catholic laity, and the institutional and hierarchical church still has to happen in the Anglo-American world.

Vatican II and Synodality:
Walking Together vs. Walking Out

The ecclesial crisis takes place in the context of a larger cultural, political, and social polycrisis.[24] For a recovery of Vatican II and, in the long run, of a healthy sense of the church, two possibilities arise to return to a reception of the council in our church—both routes requiring the leadership of the bishops, followed by the leadership of clergy, theologians, then lay leaders in this vast world that is American Catholicism.

The first possibility is theological, a necessity for recovering Vatican II in an integrated way:

- establishing a priority of documents, not just the four constitutions, but all the documents, some of which have been unjustifiably ranked as inferior (especially *Nostra Aetate* on non-Christian religions and *Dignitatis Humanae* on religious liberty);
- bringing forward the indispensable final documents of Vatican II, essential in letting the entirety of Vatican II speak in an inter-textual and dialogical way with papal teaching;

---

[24] For the origins of the term polycrisis, see Edgar Morin and Anne Brigitte Kern, *Homeland Earth: A Manifesto for the New Millenium* (Cresskill, NJ: Hampton Press, 1999).

- taking seriously the historicity of the council, not just the letter of the documents, but also the event and the spirit of the council, without separating or opposing the two (as the Extraordinary Synod of Bishops of 1985 said);
- acknowledging the issues on which Vatican II was silent or came too early, as well as acknowledging that aspects of conciliar theology require completion in ways compatible with the *modus procedendi* of the tradition. Thanks to papal teaching, this is something that has already begun to be addressed: on abuse, on women, on racism, on colonialism. This can be accomplished in honest acknowledgment without simply throwing accusations at Vatican II for being limited and recognizing the debt we owe to the council fathers, the periti, and all those who contributed to what we call Vatican II;
- remembering and honoring Vatican II without fueling veterans' sentimentality, on the one hand, or dismissing the younger generations, on the other hand. In this our theological language needs to be unapologetically conciliar, whether or not we use the label "Vatican II" in these conversations.

The second possibility for recovering an integrated Vatican II is at the level of *ecclesial life*. For this to happen it is urgent to:

- detach Vatican II from narratives that are ecclesially and politically partisan. Just as other divided groups in American Christianity need to avoid tunnel vision, "Vatican II Catholics" must stop consulting themselves for guidance;
- focus on the inclusion of minority and marginalized groups, otherwise there is no future for Vatican II and Catholicism in general. Vatican II is still perceived in the United States (and in US academia) as "the last big thing" rather then the next big thing, as it was formed from a Catholicism dominated by white European males;

- bridge the gap between bishops and theology. This is an urgent call, as the gap is not just hurting the bishops and the understanding and study of theology, but is harming the entire church;
- embrace the great opportunity in synodality to revive an inclusive, healthy sense of the church. As John O'Malley, SJ, wrote in one of his last articles: "Although Pope Francis's call is altogether traditional, it is radically new in the breadth it envisages. This should not scandalize us but energize us. We are entering upon a great project, and our responsibility for its success is as great as the project itself."[25]

As Pope Francis wrote in the preface of the book co-authored by Cardinal Michael Czerny, SJ, and Christian Barone, "It is necessary to make more explicit the key concepts of Vatican Council II, the foundations of its arguments, its theological and pastoral horizon, the arguments and the method it used."[26] Yes, Francis's pontificate is embattled, largely at the theological level, and mostly because of his recovery of the council. But this battle for the meaning of Vatican II will be with us for a long time. At stake is not just the communion with the bishop of Rome, but also the viability of the Catholic magisterial and intellectual tradition.

Catholic Higher Education and Vatican II in the Twenty-First Century

In the history of the interrupted reception of Vatican II, academic theology has played different roles in different parts of the world. It is a long and complex history that still needs to

---

[25] John W. O'Malley, "The History of Synodality: It's Older than You Think," *America*, February 17, 2022.

[26] See Christian Barone and Michael Czerny, *Siblings All, Sign of the Times: The Social Teaching of Pope Francis* (Maryknoll, NY: Orbis Books, 2022).

be written and understood in local contexts. Theology offers something profound, as it has carved out for itself a new space of freedom within a changing system of Catholic higher education, diversified its voices, and provided the magisterium with a necessary constructive criticism, especially between the pontificates of Paul VI and Benedict XVI.

Now, well into the twenty-first century, Catholic academic theology must face a new reality and make some decisions about its relationship not only with Vatican II, but more generally with the Catholic tradition. For a long time the assumed and taken-for-granted solidity of the Vatican II dispensation within the Catholic cultural and educational system allowed for a certain "conciliar agnosticism" of theologians and religious-studies scholars in Catholic institutions. There was a distance of theological academia from Vatican II, in the assumption of a vicarious cultivation of that theology of the tradition elsewhere, by someone within the church or outside of it, in culture at large.

Today, one side persists with a liberal mythology of the age of Vatican II packaged together with the 1960s "and all that" (to paraphrase the title of John O'Malley's book on Trent)[27]—the civil rights movement but also Woodstock and the sexual revolution. This mythology is often a substitute for a basic knowledge of the theology of Vatican II. On the other side there is a radical de-mythologization of Vatican II painted as the rot from which all the evils of modern religiosity flow, which presents itself as an anti-myth, when it is just another formation of myth.

The globalization of Catholicism and of the "culture wars" brings us a new chapter in the history of the battle for the meaning of Vatican II. The decision to reengage with Vatican II

---

[27] See John W. O'Malley, *Trent and All That: Renaming Catholicism in the Early Modern Era* (Cambridge, MA: Harvard University Press, 2000).

and the Catholic tradition cannot be, for academic theology, just a tactical maneuver now made possible by the room created by Pope Francis's de-escalation of the confrontation between magisterium and theologians. This theological reengagement is an act of fidelity to the synodal church, one of the fruits of Vatican II. In the church of Catholic synodality, ignorance of the conciliar tradition will make the relationship between theologians and the church even more difficult. In this, academic theology and Catholic universities have a key role to play in the decades ahead.

On the campus of Catholic colleges and universities, conciliar agnosticism will send to different kinds of students and colleagues a message promoting disengagement from the life of the church and of its theological debates. It is not infrequent to hear Catholic students express the feeling that theology and religious-studies departments on Catholic campuses are not likely places for them to find nourishment in their sense of belonging to the church. This is not just because of undeniable theological antipathies between academic theologians and the younger generations of militant Catholics, but also because of the perception of academic theology as uniquely embodying a separation between hyper-specialized scholars of religion and the living tradition of the church. The interruption of the reception of Vatican II in the last thirty years is part of a larger, unresolved problem between academic theology and the Catholic tradition, and a failure to find an alternative to both old and new forms of traditionalism and a post-ecclesial, radical deconstructivism.

This does not mean that academic theologians must become a new kind of apologist for all Catholic tradition, Vatican II, and papal magisterium. It means acknowledging the problem of an interrupted reception while participating in efforts to recover an intellectually honest and critical, but also constructive, engagement with the past—unless, that is, we have decided that the past is not just past, but also *dépassé*—deceased.[28] Such a disposition from Catholic academic theology would surely one day put our profession out of business, but even more immediately make us even more so guests in our own house—both in the church and the university.

---

[28] See Hartog, *Régimes d'historicité*, 117: with the modern regime of historicity, "le passé est, par principe ou par position, dépassé."

3

Theology
in the University

A Guest in Its Own House?

Mutual Alienation between
Different Catholic Cultures around Vatican II

The relationship between Vatican II and universities has been studied mostly in relation to matters concerning the participation of pontifical universities in the preparation of the council,[1] and less in relation to the post–Vatican II period in Catholic colleges and universities.[2] There is a great silence in the relationship between Vatican II and higher education.

In 1959 and 1960, in preparation for the council, theological faculties were invited to submit proposals for the formation of the conciliar agenda. Besides the pontifical universities in

---

[1] For example, Pasquale Bua, "La Gregoriana e il Concilio: Il contributo dei teologi dell'Università al Vaticano II," in *Gregorianum* 96, no. 2 (2015): 319–43.

[2] See James O'Toole, "The Council on Campus: The Experience of Vatican II at Boston College," *Catholic Historical Review* 103 (Summer 2017): 508–28. See also the works by Gerd-Rainer Horn on progressive European Catholicism after Vatican II.

Rome, a limited number of Catholic universities contributed to the agenda of Vatican II (only three from the United States).[3] During the council some eminent periti belonged to religious orders (especially Jesuits and Dominicans) and were professors in the institutions of theological formation for their orders, and a number of them taught at Catholic universities under episcopal oversight (for example, the nemesis of John Courtney Murray, SJ, Monsignor Joseph Fenton at Catholic University of America). But other periti (both official and unofficial) were academics in state or public universities (Joseph Ratzinger at the University of Bonn and later in Tübingen; Karl Rahner at the University of Munich; Giuseppe Alberigo at the University of Florence and later Bologna) or in Catholic universities in a system of non-separation between church and state (Edward Schillebeeckx, OP, at the Catholic University of Nijmegen in the Netherlands; Willy Onclin and Gerard Philips at the Catholic University of Leuven in Belgium).

The role of theologians at Vatican II was central, but even so, more marginal compared to previous councils, including Trent.[4] However, the council assumed a robust relationship between theology and academia. The literary genre of Vatican II texts, that is, non-legislative but narrative texts, required a sustained effort of cultural mediation among magisterium, the church, and the world that was different from the most similar predecessor of Vatican II, the Council of Trent, four centuries before.

The theology of the laity, the relationship between the church and the modern world, ecumenism and interreligious dialogue, and most of all the value attributed to the sciences and cultures—all this had in mind not an intellectualistic church, but one

---

[3] Catholic University of America in Washington, DC; St. Mary of the Lake in Chicago; and St. Mary's in Baltimore.

[4] See John W. O'Malley, *Trent: What Happened at the Council* (Cambridge, MA: Belknap Press, 2013); id., *Vatican I: The Council and the Making of the Ultramontane Church* (Cambridge, MA: Belknap Press, 2018).

still strongly informed by the world of higher education. This relationship was expressed by Paul VI in one his final messages, "Address of Pope Paul VI to Men of Thought and Science," on December 8, 1965:

> Why a special greeting for you? Because all of us here, bishops and Fathers of the council, are on the lookout for truth. What have our efforts amounted to during these four years except a more attentive search for and deepening of the message of truth entrusted to the Church and an effort at more perfect docility to the spirit of truth.
>
> Hence our paths could not fail to cross. Your road is ours. Your paths are never foreign to ours. We are the friends of your vocation as searchers, companions in your fatigues, admirers of your successes and, if necessary, consolers in your discouragement and your failures.

The collaboration between bishops and theologians at Vatican II implied a similar collaboration in the post–Vatican II period, and certainly the "Land O' Lakes Statement" of 1967 inaugurated a new era, but more for the idea of the *Catholic university* per se, rather than for *theology in Catholic universities.*

Then a rupture took place in the post-conciliar period when, in July 1968, Paul VI's encyclical *Humanae Vitae* brought an end to the honeymoon between Catholicism and modern liberal culture in the West. This was the beginning of an age of dissent that took different forms for the laity in the pews, the clergy, and academic theology. It was a dissent that, at its best, tried to distinguish carefully between different levels of authority of church teaching, attempting to articulate a loyal or faithful dissent rather than to be an assault on church teaching or papal authority as such.

It was not only *Humanae Vitae* that overshadowed the "Land O' Lakes Statement" of 1967. In 1975, *Persona Humana*, the

Congregation for the Doctrine of the Faith's "Declaration
on Certain Questions Concerning Sexual Ethics" (about ho-
mosexuality), compounded the rift between the magisterium
and Catholic theological academia. Large parts of the Catholic theological world would later adopt a view of 1990's *Ex
Corde Ecclesiae* (and also the *Catechism of the Catholic Church*
of 1992) based on the belief that John Paul II and the Vatican
were imposing an unacceptably unilateral understanding of
Catholicism on Catholic education. Claiming a rift between
academic theology and papal teaching, opposing sides infor-
mally began contesting the legacy of Vatican II. This rift was
even more consequential than the rupture with the Society of
Saint Pius X and the excommunication of Archbishop Marcel
Lefebvre in 1988.

The rift interrupting the reception of Vatican II is *not* solely
a creation of fringe traditionalism—the Society of Saint Pius X
(SSPX) and other forms of schismatic Catholicism. It is a larger
and deeper phenomenon, with roots as far back as the 1970s,
which began in parallel with the Lefebvrite schism and similar
groups between the 1970s and the 1988 excommunication of
Lefebvre.[5]

Until the mid-1980s Vatican II had a prominent role in the
documents of the United States Conference of Catholic Bishops (a role that continues in Latin American Catholicism and
elsewhere). Then, in the 1990s, something changed, even as it

---

[5] For a periodization, it is relevant to consider what Cuneo wrote in 1995.
He identified three phases in the history of post–Vatican II traditionalism in
the United States: 1962–1971, 1971–1984, 1984– . See also Michael W. Cuneo,
"Life Battles: The Rise of Catholic Militancy within the American Pro-Life
Movement," in *Being Right: Conservative Catholics in America*, ed. Mary Jo Weaver
and R. Scott Appleby, 241–69 (Bloomington: Indiana University Press, 1995),
esp. 242–47. For the traditionalist narrative on Vatican II (not only in the United
States), it is also important to recognize the role of the book by Ralph Wiltgen,
The Rhine Flows into the Tiber (1967; Rockford, IL: Tan Books, 1985).

was inseparable from the early gaps: a deeper polarization in American politics and more generally in the West. Understanding what happened in the decade of the 1990s generally informs today's situation in the church and also reflects the history of the reception of Vatican II in academic theology. In this decade the international project for a history of Vatican II developed with minimal involvement of scholars from the United States, minimizing the impact of US scholarship and the national conversation on the council.[6] That also reflects on US bishops at Vatican II, the majority of whom were not theologians, so that when the council ended, they hadn't really engaged theologians seriously. The episcopal hierarchy is partly to blame if theologians, looking to do something consequential, responded by looking outside the institution to make their mark.

Within the 1990s a process began of mutual alienation between different Catholic cultures around Vatican II. This decade records the rise of the neo-conservative theological and political project as well, including in the Catholic Church,[7] first in the world of journalism and public intellectuals, and later in academia—a long march that will bear its bitter fruits in the new millennium. In that period two different kinds of reassessments of Vatican II began. On the right, there was a theological-political, neo-conservative revision of the effects of the council in the name of an idealized past, in a defense of that recent pre-Vatican II past (one that many believed Vatican II made unusable) and against a liberal-progressive interpretation

---

[6] See *History of Vatican II*, 5 vols., ed. Giuseppe Alberigo, English version ed. Joseph A. Komonchak (Maryknoll, NY: Orbis Books, 1995–2006).

[7] See Massimo Borghesi, *Catholic Discordance: Neoconservatism vs. the Field Hospital Church of Pope Francis*, trans. Barry Hudock (Collegeville, MN: Liturgical Press, 2021); Peter Steinfels, *The Neoconservatives: The Origins of a Movement* (New York: Simon and Schuster, 1979); Damon Linker, *The Theocons: Secular America under Siege* (Albany, NY: Anchor, 2007).

of the conciliar teaching.[8] At first this happened without attacking the legitimacy of Vatican II itself. At that stage the rise of neo-conservative Catholicism was defined by a critique of the reception of Vatican II rather than as a critique of Vatican II per se. But it already expressed a theo-political critique of the conciliar teachings proceeding from a post hoc, propter hoc—an identification of Vatican II as the cause of the social and cultural disruption in the West beginning in the late 1960s.[9]

Later, beginning with the first decade of the twenty-first century and together with the changes in the national conversation about religion and politics after 9/11, this revisionism of Vatican II has became far reaching, with an attack against the theology of Vatican II, the active attempt to evict Vatican II from our common home, and later the targeting of the teaching of Pope Francis in ways that sought to delegitimize his papacy. What happened in the last few years shows that the theology of many bishops and power elites (political, financial, in the courts of law) ground to a standstill, stuck in the 1950s—with the theology of most US bishops at Vatican II, with significant exceptions regarding issues of religious liberty, dialogue with the Jews, and ecumenism.

On the other side of the spectrum, during the same thirty years a process began of hypostatization and "monumentalization" of Vatican II in a theological system where often the focus on the post-conciliar came at the expense of reliable understanding of the teaching of Vatican II itself. The ignorance was

---

[8] See Joseph Chinnici, "An Historian's Creed and the Emergence of Post-conciliar Culture Wars," *The Catholic Historical Review*, 94 no. 2 (2008): 219–44; Richard John Neuhaus, *The Catholic Moment* (San Francisco: Harper and Row, 1987).

[9] See Stephen Schloesser, "'Dancing on the Edge of the Volcano': Biopolitics and What Happened after Vatican II," in *From Vatican II to Pope Francis: Charting a Catholic Future*, ed. Paul Crowley, 3–26 (Maryknoll, NY: Orbis Books, 2014).

not just regarding the final documents of the council, but also of the historical event. While there was no direct attack against Vatican II, a silent decoupling took place in a process of estrangement from the conciliar tradition in favor of the post-conciliar, not just of a *post-confessional* nature, but also of a *post-traditional* one. This has causes that were both internal to academia (the precarious position of theology in Catholic colleges and universities; the system of academic recruitment and career) and external (understandable frustration with the perceived failure of the church to deliver on the promises of Vatican II). This indirect disqualification of Vatican II created a vacuum waiting to be filled by other theological and academic programs within higher education, outside the university, and within the church—with far-reaching effects also on seminaries for the formation of priests and religious[10]—one of the symptoms of the end, also for theology, of the monopoly and exalted status of the universities.

It was John O'Malley's *What Happened at Vatican II*—a book published in 2008 by a nonreligious academic house, Harvard University Press (and translated into numerous languages, published worldwide), during the pontificate of Benedict XVI—that helped rescue the theology of the council from oblivion, as well as from subtle forms of abrogation and delegitimization.[11] Benedict XVI, elected three years earlier, had already given clear indications and made decisions related to a revision of the institutional interpretation of Vatican II. This was revealed in multiple forms, including the famous discourse on the two conciliar hermeneutics of "continuity and reform and of discontinuity and rupture" of December 22, 2005; in his lecture at the University of Regensburg in September 2006; and again in July 2007, when

---

[10] See Katarina Schuth, *Seminary Formation: Recent History, Current Circumstances, New Directions* (Collegeville, MN: Liturgical Press, 2016).

[11] See John W. O'Malley, *What Happened at Vatican II* (Cambridge, MA: Belknap Press, 2008).

he decided the liberalization of the pre-conciliar Mass in Latin with the publication of the *motu proprio Summorum Pontificum*.

Vatican II in the
Relations between Church and University Today

In the early 2000s, John O'Malley saw an urgent need to make a new and different argument about Vatican II in the Catholic Church, where the memory of the conciliar event was often kept alive by those with a veterans' mentality that was incapable of reaching newer generations or those on the peripheries of the post–Vatican II academic establishment. By the time his book on the council came out in 2008, his questions were pointed: Where does Vatican II stand today, theologically? What is its position in academia, in the church, and in the intersections between academia and the church, but also related to the larger conversation within and about Catholicism? The issues that O'Malley raised then have acquired a new relevance in light of the changes in our ecclesial order—the rise of digital and social media, the collapse of established authorities, the dogmatization of political identities, and the politicization of religious identity in antagonistic terms, first of all against fellow Catholics.

A distinction no longer can be made or lines are blurred between *conservative Catholics* (those who endorsed the legitimacy of Vatican II even while criticizing aspects of its implementation) and *Catholic traditionalism*, as "a much more sectarian-like response to the problem of change in the Church rooted in a value-oriented repudiation of the council."[12] This blurred distinction came in with the rise of influencers and vocal groups on the internet (since the mid-1990s) and on social media platforms (since the early 2000s, but especially gaining force during Francis's pontificate).

---

[12] Cuneo, "Life Battles," 242.

Due to the influence of technology and the shared information via various media, the ecclesial divide between Vatican II sentimentality and the anti-Vatican II sentiment revealed a generational divide. The position acquired by new Catholic media (EWTN, Church Militant) boosted the outreach of this revisionism on Vatican II of both classical traditionalism and new militantism. The various schismatic voices and parties developed websites, podcasts, and YouTube channels that now expanded their originally marginal outreach, reaching beyond the smaller networks and beyond North America. The mutation has been made possible also by a development in other, related topics that further widened the gap: from sexual morality to bioethics to gender and identity politics. With these the influencer groups and channels received a boost—ideologically, but also sociologically and demographically—by the continuing the abortion debate from the 2010s and by debate on same-sex marriage and LGBTQ rights in society, in the law, and in the church; as well as, in the 2020s, the debate on the role of government and science in the health crisis brought about by the COVID-19 pandemic.

But the change regarding how people viewed theology as it related to Vatican II came about not only due to changing technology. The pervasive issue of the credibility of Vatican II came in light of disruptions within the last twenty years—especially the sex-abuse crisis. This has benefited one side of the ideological spectrum, where redrawing the lines regarding Vatican II has been one of the ways politically conservative Catholicism has aligned itself to one ideological side of the United States's two-party system, entailing deep changes in the ways the new generations of leaders (clerical, intellectual, business leaders) understand the concept of Catholic tradition.[13] Catholic public

---

[13] See Massimo Faggioli, *Joe Biden and Catholicism in the United States* (New London, CT: Bayard, 2021).

intellectuals, politicians, the business world, and philanthropic circles are increasingly represented by neo-traditionalist Catholics with a markedly negative or derisive view of Vatican II. Among the paradoxes in this sea change is that Catholic anti-liberalism gained access to liberal mainstream media, thanks to the appeal to ideological "diversity." In this moment, "anti-Vatican II, anti-liberal Catholics" have in the public square a platform denied or no longer relevant for "Vatican II Catholics."

What happened in the national conversation on Catholicism and politics has at the same time left academia behind as a perceived irrelevance—despite, or exactly because of, its attempts to stay relevant. This has directly affected the church and Catholic universities. The political and ideological polarization at the national level has effects on the theological dispositions toward Vatican II in our church and in our universities—a church whose most influential voices seem divided between ones holding a nostalgia for the conformist 1950s and those longing for a radical post-ecclesial Christianity that doesn't always take into account concrete ecclesial and ecclesiastical realities.

This split aggravated the pre-existing situation of the knowledge of conciliar theology and history. The *koine* on Vatican II is not just popularization, but worse, especially on the right side of "brand Catholicism" where conciliar theology is seen as heretical or, at best, as something that must be tamed and understood as purified from a hermeneutic in light of the contributions from the global church and feminist theology.[14] A simple browser

---

[14] See *The Word on Fire Vatican II Collection*, foreword by Bishop Robert Barron and commentary by the postconciliar popes (Washington, DC: Word on Fire, 2021), which includes John XXIII's *Gaudet Mater Ecclesia* of October 11, 1962, and the closing address of Vatican II by Pope Paul VI of December 7, 1965. But the collection focuses only on the four constitutions (*Dei Verbum, Lumen Gentium, Sacrosanctum Concilium,* and *Gaudium et Spes*) to the exclusion of all other documents, and it states its hermeneutical preference for John Paul II and Benedict XVI and its opposition to liberal-progressive interpretations.

search for videos or lectures on Vatican II can easily lead a person to spiritual desolation.

This is part of a larger process of the de-theologization of clerical leadership and of a distancing from the university system in favor of other institutions of education. Catholic theological education shaped by neo-traditionalist persuasions in the United States has migrated out of mainstream Catholic colleges and universities and has established new institutions funded by private donors. The theological culture at the center of their foundations shows in the ways they appeal to students through different forms of diplomatic distancing, blunt rejection, or insurgency against the mainstream reception of Vatican II in the United States, if not sometimes against conciliar teaching itself.

Moreover, the changes in what stands in for "Catholic" in many Catholic universities includes the influence of media, journalism, the monopoly of the Catholic appeal by disciplines other than theology, and the "think-tankization" of scholarship. This also means more and more trained theologians are working outside of academia but not directly for the church either[15]— ending the "golden age" of academic theology.[16]

The paradox is that the mechanisms for disciplining and controlling academic Catholic theology implemented by Rome after Vatican II were the result of a delusion that intended to solve one problem in the United States, but created a bigger one, marginalizing academic theology from the *ecclesia* while also favoring the spread of a pseudo-theological or non-theological (journalistic) culture with key platforms and a national-global internet audience. In 1958, Italian journalist, novelist, and playwright (including of

---

[15] See Matthew Shadle, "Can You Be a Theologian outside of Academia? I'm Going to Find Out," *America*, March 15, 2023.

[16] At the annual meeting of the Catholic Theological Society of America in June 2023, Frank Clooney's presidential plenary acknowledged the end of a past "golden era" in which the discipline of theology thrived in Catholic universities across the country.

Federico Fellini's films) Ennio Flaiano described French Catholicism as "a literary movement."[17] One could say that in the public
square of twenty-first-century America, the Catholic debate is
largely a journalistic movement that leaves theologians (and bishops) on the margins, left to comment on the work of Catholic
political voices, activists, judges, and donors.

The fragmentation of the initiatives today corresponds with a
pulverization of research, teaching, and academic cultures. There
is a fragmentation within conservative Catholicism, the rise of
the "trads" and "integralists" that makes mainstream 1990s neoconservatism less dominant. But there is also the rise of new
centers for the Catholic intellectual tradition in non-Catholic
colleges and universities that compete for the attention of young
Catholic intellectuals, who often struggle to find what they are
looking for in departments of theology and/or religious studies
in Catholic colleges and universities.

Then there are other theological enterprises (like the Lumen
Christi Institute at the University of Chicago) steering clear of
the culture-war traditionalism, but also of Vatican II Catholicism—from what it is or has become. This "non-conciliar, and
non-anticonciliar" culture has taken root also in mainstream
colleges and universities and in specialized, para-university institutes populated by Catholic thinkers.[18] "Non-conciliar, and

[17] Ennio Flaiano (1910–72), *Diario degli errori* (Milan: Adelphi, 2022 [1976]),
33.

[18] See, for example, the In Lumine Network, led by the Lumen Christi
Institute at the University of Chicago, which includes six initial members: Lu-
men Christi, Nova Forum at the University of Southern California, Collegium
Institute for Catholic Thought and Culture at the University of Pennsylvania,
Saint Anselm Institute at the University of Virginia, COLLIS at Cornell
University, and the Harvard Catholic Forum at Harvard University. In February 2022, the Lumen Christi Institute was awarded $3,648,000 by the John
Templeton Foundation for "a three-year project that will create the first-ever
national network of independent institutes of Catholic thought, located at some
of the country's top universities. The project is called 'In Lumine: Supporting
the Catholic Intellectual Tradition on Campuses Nationwide.'"

non-anticonciliar" may be a solution to avoid the culture wars, but with long-term costs for the understanding of the tradition as it tries to isolate a particular slice of the Catholic intellectual tradition and treat it as somehow untouched by the history of the effects of doctrinal changes in the church over the past century.

At the very delicate junction between church and university, Catholic theology finds itself in a system of global research and teaching, in particular in the Western world, which is more and more selective and competitive; it presupposes a growing schizophrenia between micro-specializations and grandiose visions; it requires faith in the corporate mission at the expense of the transcendent; it designs everything and quantifies everything. The challenge for Catholic universities is enormous, moreso as boundaries are falling (at least in the Western world, where in the past they have long formed minds and spaces): between public and private universities, between profit and non-profit, between confessional and non-confessional, between advocacy and supposedly neutral academic entities.

Within the church, Catholic universities reflect a growing plurality and fragmentation. There is no longer a clear intersection between the withdrawal option and the engagement option—or even a sense that an intersection can exist, failing to engage our usual theological-political fault lines. Some Catholic colleges and universities are tempted to appeal to a more coherent identity as a persecuted minority, or they identify with one cultural or political movement, with a religious order, with a particular ecclesial agenda. Other Catholic universities, the majority in the mainstream, are attracted to a less distinct identity in their attempt to merge the contradictory identities of all. But this attempt to keep the "Catholic" as universal has become much more complicated in a culture that rewards the market of identity. The very definition of a *Catholic university* has become increasingly difficult to spell out and generate consensus among the very ones who work in them and support them.

At the intersection between academia and the church, the crisis of the theological tradition and transmission of Vatican II is a symptom of the crisis of a select minority in the church, that is, intellectuals, who have never been very good at talking with people in the pews, but lately have also stopped talking to the clerical and episcopal elites who, mutually, are not eager to see theologians as part of the ecclesial conversation.

Then there is the papacy. Catholic theology pays the price of a largely still ultramontane church that considers the popes (one pope only, of their choosing) the legal executors of the will of Vatican II. Pope Francis has revived Vatican II in many ways and on many issues. But now within the church the Catholic theological project finds itself, in terms of church politics, between the Scylla of the German pope, criticized on the one hand as the theologian who stifled theological debate, and the Charybdis of the Argentine pope, criticized by others as the "street priest" from the Global South who does not seem to have a place for academic theology in the church as a "field hospital."

Pope Francis, Theology, and
Catholic Colleges and Universities

Pope Francis has not engaged theologians as directly (and not controversially) as his predecessors coming from an academic background.[19] But he has sent unmistakable direct and indirect

---

[19] There was a close relationship between Montini/Paul VI and FUCI (Federazione Universitari Cattolici Italiani) and the Università Cattolica del Sacro Cuore in Milan. Karol Wojtyla was a professor of moral philosophy at the Catholic University of Lublin in Poland; as John Paul II he issued the *motu proprio* "Beata Hedvigis" in 1981, officially reestablishing the theological faculty of the Jagiellonian University (Poland) as the Pontifical Academy of Theology. Joseph Ratzinger/Benedict XVI maintained a well-known relationship with the universities (both Catholic and state universities) even after leaving academic life to become a bishop, cardinal and pope.

messages to theologians during the entire pontificate.[20] Among the direct messages is his letter of March 3, 2015, "To the Grand Chancellor of the Pontificia Universidad Católica Argentina for the 100th Anniversary of the Founding of the Faculty of Theology," in which he writes:

> Do not settle for a desktop theology. Your place for reflection is the frontier. Do not fall into the temptation to embellish, to add fragrance, to adjust them to some degree and domesticate them. Even good theologians, like good shepherds, have the odour of the people and of the street and, by their reflection, pour oil and wine onto the wounds of mankind.
>
> Theology is an expression of a church which is a "field hospital," which lives her mission of salvation and healing in the world. Mercy is not just a pastoral attitude but it is the very substance of the Gospel of Jesus. I encourage you to study how the various disciplines—dogma, morality, spirituality, law, and so on—may reflect the centrality of mercy.
>
> Without mercy our theology, our law, our pastoral care run the risk of collapsing into bureaucratic narrow-mindedness or ideology, which by their nature seeks to domesticate the mystery. Understanding theology is understanding God, who is Love.

On October 1, 2017, Pope Francis visited the University of Bologna. Believed to have been established in 1088, Bologna is said

---

[20] See other speeches of Francis to Catholic universities: February 9, 2017, to the participants in the plenary of the Vatican Congregation for Catholic Education; October 31, 2019, to the conference in Rome, New Frontiers for University Leaders: The Future of Health and the University Ecosystem; November 26, 2019, to Sophia University in Tokyo; September 29, 2022, address at the conference Initiatives in Refugee and Migrant Education; February 25, 2023, to the Pontifical Universities in Rome; May 4, 2023, to a delegation from the Organization of Catholic Universities of Latin America and the Caribbean; August 2, 2023, to the Catholic University of Portugal.

to be the oldest university in the Western world. Now a secular university in the Italian system of higher education dominated by state universities, Bologna played a special role in the history of universities and theology in the Middle Ages. In his speech to students and faculty at Bologna on October 1, 2017, Francis talked about the role of the university in our divided world: "The identity to which one belongs is that of the common home, of the *universitas*. The word *universitas* contains the idea of the *whole* and that of the *community*."

In his speech in Bologna, Francis briefly mentioned the relationship between the role of the university and "our common home," referencing *Laudato Si'*. That encyclical to some extent plays the role that *Gaudium et Spes* did in the immediate post-conciliar church: a vision for the role of the church in the world contending with the emergencies of the time.

Laudato Si' has become part of the syllabi at many Catholic universities, getting a better reception there than from the US bishops. Yet that reception still seems rooted in the notion that *Laudato Si'* is an encyclical only on the environment, when in fact it is also, maybe more so, a document on political power and knowledge. *Laudato Si'* speaks to the issue of technology, "which, linked to business interests, is presented as the only way of solving these problems, in fact proves incapable of seeing the mysterious network of relations between things and so sometimes solves one problem only to create others" (LS, no. 20). It goes on to denounce the distorted connections between politics, economic interests, and the manipulation of information (LS, no. 54). It criticizes the divinization of the market economy (LS, no. 56). *Laudato Si'* reminds Catholics of the foundational concept of the "common destination of goods" for a truly Catholic understanding of private property (LS, nos. 93–94). It restates the key role of government in the protection and promotion of the common good (LS, no. 157), the role of the state and of legislation, and the need to defend society, through the role of local and national political systems, from economic interests (LS, nos. 177, 189, 196). *Laudato Si'* is a call to "generate alternative solutions for our problems of today."[21]

In the apostolic constitution *Veritatis Gaudium* on ecclesiastical universities and faculties of December 8, 2017, Francis talked about the responsibilities of theology to the world:

> Theology must doubtless be rooted and grounded in sacred Scripture and in the living tradition, but for this very reason it must simultaneously accompany cultural and social processes, and particularly difficult transitions. Indeed, at this time theology must address conflicts: not only those that we experience within the Church but also those that concern the world as a whole.

But he also quoted Paul VI on the relations between theology and church: "The task of the theologian is carried out with a view to building up ecclesial communion so that the People of God may grow in the experience of faith."[22]

In his *Speech to the Pontifical Theological Faculty of Southern Italy—San Luigi section—of Naples* on June 21, 2019, Francis talked about the need for a renewal of schools of theology to have a "theology of welcoming and dialogue":

> The renewal of schools of theology comes about through the practice of discernment and through *a dialogical way of proceeding* capable of creating a corresponding spiritual environment and intellectual practice. It is a dialogue both

---

[21] See also the opening paragraph of the speech Francis gave during the audience with the Community of the Catholic University of Portugal on October 26, 2017.

[22] Quotation of Paul VI, letter to the Rector of the Catholic University of Louvain, *"Le transfert à Louvain-la-Neuve,"* September 13, 1975, in *L'Osservatore Romano*, September 22–23, 1975.

in the understanding of the problems and in the search for ways to resolve them. A dialogue capable of integrating the living criterion of Jesus's Paschal Mystery with that of analogy, which discovers connections, signs, and theological references in reality, in creation and in history. This involves the hermeneutical integration of the mystery of the path of Jesus which led him to the cross and to the resurrection and gift of the Spirit. Integrating this paschal logic of Jesus is indispensable for understanding how historical and created reality is challenged by the revelation of the mystery of God's love. Of that God who manifests himself in the history of Jesus—in every circumstance and difficulty—as greater in love and in his capacity to rectify evil.

Both movements are necessary and complementary: a *bottom-up* movement that can dialogue, with an attitude of listening and discernment, with every human and historical instance, taking into account the breadth of what it means to be human; and a *top-down* movement where "the top" is that of Jesus lifted up on the cross that allows, at the same time, to discern the signs of the Kingdom of God in history and to understand prophetically the signs of the anti-Kingdom that disfigure the soul and human history. It is a method that allows us in a dynamic that is ongoing to confront ourselves with every human condition and to grasp what Christian light can illuminate the folds of reality and what efforts the Spirit of the Risen Crucified One is arousing, from time to time, here and now.

On November 1, 2023, in the *motu proprio Ad theologiam promovendam* Francis approved the new statutes of the Pontifical Academy of Theology.[23] Francis called for a "cultural revolution":

---

[23] Translations from Italian of the *motu proprio* in this section are the author's.

a more contextual theology, talking to and receiving from the people of God, less abstract and more pastoral. He defined theology as "true critical knowledge as sapiential knowledge, not abstract and ideological, but spiritual, elaborated on our knees, shaped by adoration and prayer," a knowledge that cannot "forget its sapiential/wisdom dimension." The *motu proprio* calls theologians to be more contextual but this implies also a more incarnational, embodied, and testimonial view of the profession—which is very difficult or impossible to incorporate in a job description for a new position or for the evaluation of the accomplishments of a Catholic theologian. Francis said that theology must develop "in a culture of dialogue and encounter between different traditions and different knowledge, between different Christian confessions and different religions, openly discussing with everyone, believers and non-believers." He also encouraged theology to be dialogical and interdisciplinary, but also communal:

> Dialogue with other forms of knowledge evidently presupposes dialogue within the ecclesial community and awareness of the essential synodal and communion dimension of doing theology: the theologian cannot help but experience fraternity and communion firsthand, at the service of evangelization and to reach everyone's heart. . . . It is therefore important that there exist places, including institutional ones, in which to live and experience collegiality and theological fraternity.

A New "Land O' Lakes Statement" for Theology in the Twenty-First Century

Issued in the summer of 1967, the "Land O' Lakes Statement" reimagined a new path for Catholic higher education in the

United States.[24] While similar discussions were taking place in Colombia, France, and the Philippines under the auspices of the International Federation of Catholic Universities, Catholic higher education in the United States had at the time (as now) an exceptional strength and rooted presence in comparison to the rest of the world. The importance of the "Land O' Lakes Statement" became visible much later than in the late 1960s, at which time the document was seen as one of the many in the post-conciliar turmoil.[25] The renewed attention to it is part of the ongoing intra-Catholic "culture wars."

Almost sixty years later the "Land O' Lakes Statement" is attacked as much as it is celebrated, reliably cited in the anti-Vatican II reaction of the most vocal neo-conservative and neo-traditionalist circles of American Catholicism, including the Cardinal Newman Society and the magazine *First Things*.[26] It has also aged. Firmly rooted in the conciliar theological vision of the role of the church in the modern world—the pastoral constitution *Gaudium et Spes* much more than the conciliar decree on education *Gravissimum Educationis*—the "Land O' Lakes Statement" needs an update. But it is not clear if, when, or even how there might be another such meeting of leaders in American Catholic higher education.

The challenge is in finding common ground. In the almost sixty years since Fr. Ted Hesburgh convened the Land O' Lakes conference, differences among Catholic colleges and universities

---

[24] See Michael Hahn, "The University: The Catholic University in the Modern World," in *Hesburgh of Notre Dame: Assessments of a Legacy*, ed. Todd C. Ream and Michael J. James (Cham Switzerland: Palgrave Macmillan, 2023), 41–67.

[25] See David J. O'Brien, *From the Heart of the American Church: Catholic Higher Education and American Culture* (Maryknoll, NY: Orbis Books, 1994).

[26] See William Dempsey, "Notre Dame's Deal with the Devil," *First Things*, August 4, 2016; and Richard Maggi, "Hesburgh and Rice," *First Things*, March 20, 2015.

have grown. There's a wider gap between top research universities and small liberal-arts colleges. There's a widening diversity along the cultural spectrum within Catholicism, and more ideological polarization, with campuses reflecting these differences. Catholic identities and missions are in flux; while religious-cultural wars play out in theology departments, there is otherwise a general indifference to theology elsewhere on Catholic campuses, and at some schools, traditional theology and philosophy course requirements are being reduced or eliminated. There are significantly fewer women religious among faculties, and a growing number of lay women in higher education. Departments of theology and religious studies in Catholic universities have embraced ecumenism and interreligious theology, where Catholic faculty often are a minority in those departments—and there is a significant diversity between different interpretations of Catholicism among Catholic faculty. And, of course, more institutions historically run by religious orders are gradually giving way to lay leadership.

In the age of the "Land O' Lakes Statement," Catholic higher education in the United States expected a transition from clerical/religious boards of trustees to lay boards of trustees, where what happened instead was actually a takeover by corporate boards of trustees, resulting in that sense of Catholic mission of those universities depending more and more on the personal convictions of board members who come from different professions and different cultures—often foreign to (and sometimes mildly contemptuous of) theology, the humanities, and the liberal arts in general. This development in the governance of Catholic colleges and universities in the United States is instructive for those who think diversifying top leadership appointees for ecclesiastical administration (with a growing number of lay people governing parishes, dioceses, schools, hospitals—but also the Roman Curia) automatically suggests some kind of progress.

A new "Land O' Lakes Statement" for theology, in light of
Francis's pontificate, would thus be important—not because of
the prospect of the unknown of the next pontificate, but rather
because his papacy signals an epochal shift in global Catholicism
and therefore US Catholicism. Francis embodies a new relationship between *propositional* Catholicism and *testimonial* Catholicism—something that challenges both liberal and conservative
takes on the relationship between higher education and the
institutional church. Liberal Catholic theologians should see as a
thing of the past the last three decades when the doctrinal policy
of John Paul II and Benedict XVI constituted a big obstacle in
the relationship between academic theology and the magisterium. There seems to be little consensus beyond valuing critical
thinking regarding religion and culture, and even less regarding
the value of "Catholic" and "ecclesial."

There is no Catholic tradition without Catholic social
thought, but the Catholic tradition is more than Catholic social thought. On the other side of our polarized Catholicism,
the language of Francis on life issues and its refusal to use the
rhetoric of non-negotiable values makes it apparently impossible
for neo-conservative, traditionalist, and "orthodox" Catholicism
to acknowledge the evangelical and missionary aspects of this
pontificate and its potential for the culture of Catholic educators.

There are challenges and profound questions as to the role of
the Catholic colleges and universities in evangelization. Catholic
higher education could be expected to be a part of the church's
mission to evangelize. As James Heft puts it:

> As long as we understand that evangelization in the uni-
> versity context is not proselytization, that it respects the
> integrity of the academic disciplines, focuses on the search
> for truth in its research and teaching, gives special attention
> in its research and teaching to expanding knowledge that

serves the common good, and keeps moral and religious questions in the awareness of the faculty.[27]

What is not clear today is whether Catholic theological academia still sees itself with an ecclesial role, cooperating in building the Catholic tradition in subdisciplines that are other than Catholic social thought. Francis has said little on Catholic higher education directly, but a reception (or depending on the viewpoint, non-reception) of his ecclesiology would impact the future of Catholic colleges and universities. Reception would likely help correct some misperceptions on the real challenges facing Catholic higher education. The debate on the legacy of the "Land O' Lakes Statement" tends to focus on issues of Catholic identity and (or versus) mission, in a political-ecclesiological framework largely centered on the issue of the relationship between Catholic institutions of higher education and the institutional church—the papacy and the bishops.

In this respect, Francis's pontificate has interacted less than his predecessors with the world of universities, perhaps in part because of the reluctance of Francis's anti-elitism to engage in a dialogue with academics. Pope Francis's repeated references to the risk of self-isolation and social exclusivity of academics are more than just a riff on his original view of the church as a "field hospital."[28]

However, Francis's theology and ecclesiology is richly suggestive for the future of Catholic higher education, and particularly responsive in facing the challenges of today, primarily related to

---

[27] James L. Heft, *The Future of Catholic Higher Education: The Open Circle* (New York: Oxford University Press, 2021), 88.

[28] See Massimo Faggioli, "Theology between the University and the Church as a 'Field Hospital,'" in *Theology and the University*, ed. Fáinche Ryan, Dirk Ansorge, and Josef Quitterer (Abingdon, Oxfordshire: Routledge, 2024), 39–54.

the survival of the idea of the university as a community that believes in the education of the whole human person, not one enslaved to a technocratic paradigm. In this project *academic* theology has a role that cannot be rejected. As Zena Hitz phrases it: "Learning and intellectual life are not exclusive province of professional academics, but academics are their official guardians; and so a good place to begin renewal from."[29]

Francis helps us see either way that the university is part of a social, political, and economic context much larger than the relationship between Catholic academia and institutional Catholicism. Universities are not and should not be the intellectual counterpart of the institutional church of the bishops—*studium* (education and scholarship) vis-à-vis *sacerdotium* (the clergy). Universities are also part of a constitutional view of our common home, where key pillars remain: political power (*regnum*), society, and the market economy. In this sense the debate on the future of the "Land O' Lakes Statement" for theology requires at least three areas of focus.

The first focal point is the *ecclesiological*. A lot has changed in Catholic higher education since 1967. In addition to the factors mentioned above, there is also now a wider gap between academic theology and the magisterium; stronger opposition to the idea of Catholic (including pontifical) universities serving as institutions of higher education for ecclesial movements like Opus Dei, the Legionaries of Christ, and Focolare; and a greater tendency to move research from universities to privately funded think-tanks with specific political-economic agendas, such as the Acton Institute. And there is now also the question of the role of church authority in higher education.

Yet the real ecclesiological question still lingers: just what is the real constitutional role of Catholic universities in the

---

[29] Zena Hitz, *Lost in Thought: The Hidden Pleasures of an Intellectual Life* (Princeton, NJ: Princeton University Press, 2020), 48.

Catholic Church? The Boston College conference on *Amoris Laetitia* of October 2016 gives us one possible example. A different one is given in Catholic University of America's invitation to Charles Koch to speak on "good profit" in October 2017.

A second and more urgent area of focus is the *political*. Is the politics of knowledge expressed by the "Land O' Lakes Statement" still adequate? At the very beginning, in the first paragraph, the "Land O' Lakes Statement" declares that "the Catholic university must have a true autonomy and academic freedom in the face of authority of whatever kind, lay or clerical, external to the academic community itself." There is no question that Catholic colleges and universities have acquired a remarkable autonomy from ecclesiastical institutions; this is something that should be treasured. At the same time, it should also be reexamined in light of Pope Francis's missionary ecclesiology, especially in *Evangelii Gaudium*.

Third, and still more urgent, is the *intellectual* question: who really threatens the true autonomy and academic freedom of Catholic higher education and of theology today? In light of the crisis of the humanities and of all that does not directly meet the demands of the market, an exclusive focus on the relationship between the university and the bishops largely misses the point—or becomes an expedient alibi. Corporatization of the university, threats to academic freedom, the disappearance of tenure-track positions, and reliance on (if not exploitation of) an adjunct workforce are more worrisome than the dreaded intrusions of the magisterium or the local bishops. The reshaping of the university is well within the reach of the wealthy and the politicians who shape universities through political power and the lavishing of money.

Certainly bishops cannot presume to determine what should and should not be taught in the university today. But the question is, for academic theologians, to open the eyes to others—social, political, and corporate leaders—who already, in more

subtle ways, determine that and decide what theology's responsibility to the church is—the church as a people, a community,
and as an institution.

The way in which powerful, wealthy Catholic universities
strike a balance in their relationship with a weaker institutional
church isn't an indication of or a recipe for the solution of a
bigger problem. If there is to be an update of the "Land O' Lakes
Statement," the real starting point would be to learn where leaders in American Catholic higher education really stand on the
increasing marketization and politicization of knowledge and on
the role of theology in the university.

Moving beyond the Intra-Catholic Fights

In 1996, Carmel Elizabeth McEnroy published a book on
women in the church of Vatican II titled *Guests in Their Own
House*.[30] Since it was written, the issue of the role of women in
the church has not visibly shifted, though recently hope, especially in the context of synodality and the synodal process, has
been important, even though Catholic universities and colleges
in the United States have been largely absent from that process,
not entirely by their own fault.

But there is an interesting paradox here. While some post–
Vatican II issues have made progress in the church (care for creation, women in the church, a less Europe-centered and Rome-
centered Catholicism, among others), the theology of Vatican II
itself seems to be more and more a "guest in its own house." But
without a Catholic theology based on Vatican II supporting those
advancements, they could have a very short life.

This is a problem not just for Vatican II theologians or for
experts of Vatican II. It is a problem for supporting a healthy

---

[30] See Carmel Elizabeth McEnroy, *Guests in Their Own House: The Women
of Vatican II* (New York: Crossroad, 1996).

sense of a tradition; we do not want to fall into the denial of historical development as a Catholic form of receiving God's revelation. But it is a problem also for those progressives who think Vatican II is passé, in the no-man's land between the Middle Ages and postmodernity, and that conciliar teaching is an *adiaphoron*—something neither forbidden nor required—because they have embraced social justice Catholicism. In other words, a *non-Vatican II* or *a-Vatican II* theology could put in danger those same social-political issues (especially diversity and inclusion) about which the Catholic theological academic establishment cares deeply.

The question is this: How sustainable are the post–Vatican II advancements in our understanding of the gospel without a firm anchoring in Vatican II itself and in the idea of the living tradition as articulated by Vatican II? What has happened during the pontificate of Pope Francis, especially in the church in the United States, has something to tell us about the consequences of a detachment from, even more than a *revanche* against, that fundamental event in the history of the Catholic tradition.

One of the side effects and unexpected consequences of the "order" of the "Land O' Lakes Statement" and of the epistemological shift that the liberal arts have experienced toward political activism has been the internal displacement of departments of theology and religious studies in many Catholic universities— not just displacement from the center of campus life, but also displacement from a certain sense of their own mission. It is not unheard of that committed, practicing Catholic undergrads are able to pick up on the intra-Catholic ideological battles that we faculty may be responding to in our research, resulting in their coming away with the impression that the Catholic faculty are actively anti-Catholic or somehow hostile to the faith they know and grew up with.

This is not just a problem for every effective marketing strategy of our theology programs to students. It is also of a

problem of coherence and consistency in the eyes of the university community and of the ecclesial communion, as well as
of those who witness the work of these programs: non-Catholic,
non-Christian, and nonbeliever colleagues, students, staff, alumni,
and donors, stretching also to the church and the public square.

4

De-Theologization and Catholic Higher Education

Synods, Seminaries, and Campuses

What Role Do Catholic Colleges and Universities Have in a Synodal Church?

The role of Catholic colleges and universities in the life of the church is more and more uncertain. This was evident in the text of the "Synthesis Report" of the first assembly of the XVI General Ordinary Assembly of the Synod of Bishops, October 4–29, 2023:

i) It is necessary to continue ecclesial reflection on the original interweaving of love and truth flowing from Christological revelation, with a view to an ecclesial practice faithful to these origins.

ii) We encourage experts in different fields to bring together their knowledge with their personal spirituality so that what they offer is a real ecclesial service. What synodality means in this context is a readiness to think together in the service of mission and in diverse settings, but with a shared sense of purpose.

iii) We identified a need for reflection on the conditions that enable theological and cultural research that takes as its starting point the daily experience of God's Holy People and places itself at its service. (no. 15)

In a church that wants and tries to be, as Pope Francis repeatedly emphasized, "open to all, all, all," Catholic colleges and universities are hardly an exception in the contemporary moment, when universities have become or risk becoming sects of the privileged—a paradox for Catholicism, which is the antithesis of sectarianism.

One example of the changing relationship between Catholic colleges and universities and the church is the synodal process opened by Pope Francis in 2021. The synodal process has involved (or at least invited) all local churches to participate. But if you spent part of your life on the campus of a Catholic college or university—as a student, teacher, member of the staff, parent—in the years of the synodal process, you could easily miss how the church was in the middle of the biggest ecclesial event since the Second Vatican Council and how it was meant to involve the entire people of God.

The apparent mutual indifference between the synodal process and the Catholic higher-educational institutions deserves comparison to the time of Vatican II. During the preparation of Vatican II (1959–60), theological faculties were invited to submit their proposals for the formation of the conciliar agenda (for the United States: Catholic University of America, St. Mary of the Lake in Chicago, and St. Mary's in Baltimore).[1] The participation of most members of university communities at Vatican II

---

[1] See *Acta et Documenta Concilio Oecumenico Vaticano II Apparando. Series I (Antepraeparatoria). Volumen IV: Studia et Vota Universitatum et Facultatum Ecclesiasticarum et Catholicarum. Pars II: Universitates et Facultates extra Urbem* (Città del Vaticano: Typis Polyglottis Vaticanis, 1961), 617–49.

was remote: as observers through the mass media, even though some of the most influential theological advisers at Vatican II had chairs in Catholic and pontifical universities. Among the messages delivered on the last day of Vatican II, there was no specific message for students at colleges and universities, only one for youth in general.[2]

But in the immediate post-conciliar period the universities' participation in Vatican II picked up. The celebration and reception of Vatican II saw key participation of college and university students and faculty, including in the United States.[3] In other countries as well the impulses of Vatican II for theological and ecclesial reform were part of a more general movement of reform—not just ecclesial in nature, but social and political too. The tumultuous post–Vatican II in theological faculties in Germany famously shocked Joseph Ratzinger (the future Benedict XVI) and convinced him to move from the University of Tübingen to the quieter University of Regensburg in his native Bavaria in 1968.[4]

Nothing like that is now occurring between academic theology and the synodal process, at least in North America. In the preparation for the synodal process launched by Pope Francis in October 2021, there was no special attention paid to students and universities—except for some media events featuring Pope Francis speaking with select groups of students via video. The presentation of the program of the synodal process in April 2021 mentioned a way to submit contributions before April 2022, but at least in the American Catholic universities the participation

---

[2] "Message of the Second Vatican Council to Youth," December 7, 1965.

[3] See James M. O'Toole, "The Council on Campus: The Experience of Vatican II at Boston College," *The Catholic Historical Review* 103, no. 3 (2017): 508–28.

[4] About 1968 in German universities and theology, see Peter Neuner, *Turbulenter Aufbruch: Die 60er Jahre zwischen Konzil und konservativer Wende* (Freiburg: Herder, 2019).

to the synod was marginal and left to the initiative of individual faculty members, students, and campus ministry.[5] In the "Vademecum" published by the Bishops' Synod in September 2022 there was a vague mention of the role of school and universities in the listening phase at the diocesan level related to the role of the bishop.[6] Even though eminent theologians (women and men, lay and clergy) were appointed as experts by the Bishops' Synod, very little attention was actually given to the importance of the contribution of the global Catholic theological and academic community to the development of synodality.

Francis has often encouraged young people to be active in the church, shake things up, and "make a mess," but students of Catholic colleges and universities did not seem to have a specific place or role in the synodal process, other than the largely symbolic appointment of students as voting members in the two assemblies of the Synod (October 2023 and October 2024). There was reluctance or delay by the national bishops' conferences and the Bishops' Synod in Rome to invite Catholic universities—not just the theologians, but students, faculty, the entire community—to take part in the synodal process. This oversight indicates several things about the synodal process, the church, and universities today.

Francis has been very clear throughout his pontificate in his encouragement for social and ecclesial movements, even as he has also kept the academic world at arm's length. Rather than being a sign of anti-intellectualism, it is rather a distrust of all

---

[5] Office of the Synod in the Vatican, "Note of the Synod of Bishops," May 21, 2021: "The Dicasteries of the Roman Curia, the University—Faculties of Theology, the Union of Superiors General—International Union Superiors General (USG—UISG) and other Unions and Federations of Consecrated life, and international lay movements, shall also provide their own contributions to the General Secretariat of the Synod of Bishops."

[6] Office of the Synod in the Vatican, "Vademecum for the Synod on Synodality," September 2021, paragraphs 3.1. and 4.1.

elites. Universities are still identified as a separate world housing the power of the experts. The synodal process is meant to rebalance power in the church, not just between lay and clergy, but also between the elites and the people.

Universities are still an important place for the church to do its thinking, and the beginning of the synodal process seemed barely interested in them—and vice versa. Many bishops do not seem to have a clear idea of what synodality is, even as Catholic academic theology is not very interested in offering courses in ecclesiology with attention to the institutional dimension of the church.[7] This distance between Catholic universities and the synodal process is a worrying symptom of a growing disconnect.

This symptom should lead us to ask questions about the larger health of the relationship between Catholic universities and the church in the ongoing ecclesial conversation. What kind of contribution of ideas and experiences can come from these institutions where shared governance is in crisis and technocratic mentality has taken over? There is clericalism in the church and there is another kind of clericalism in the universities, where the power of administrators is no less significant than the power of the clergy in the church. The real priestly caste in the university today is made up of the administrators and the donors, and not the professoriat—not just in terms of political power, but also of status and social role.

If the presidents of Catholic colleges and universities were all still members of the clergy, perhaps these institutions would have been more interested in synodality. The transition in Catholic universities to lay presidents and administrators has paradoxically contributed to the lack of interest of these institutions in an ecclesiology that proposes to give more voice to

---

[7] There are some notable exceptions, such as the program of the open course "Synod and Synodality" at the Pontifical Gregorian University and the online courses organized by Rafael Luciani at Boston College.

lay people. This is one of the cases in which the post–Vatican II transition from clerical to lay leadership in Catholic education has been a mixed blessing. On top of this corporatization of the universities, the lack of interest of many academic theologians in synodality is part of the marginal role of theology in Catholic universities. In an ecclesial situation where the pontificate of Francis has been embattled from day one, and many militant bishops show little or no interest in synodality, there has been weak institutional response from the organizations of the Catholic theologians on this front. Catholic scholarship has provided important contributions on the theology of synodality, but there has been scant organized, institutional effort to claim a place at the table—perhaps still waiting for an official invitation from the bishops' conferences or the Bishops' Synod. Moreover, in institutions of higher education the "Great Resignation" for faculty often takes shape as disengagement; there is no reason to believe that Catholic colleges and universities are exempt from this disengagement, which is happening at exactly the same time as the call to walk together in synodal form and the reform of the church.[8] Disengagement from the university community might well be piling up on disengagement from the ecclesial community.

If synodality cannot manage getting young people interested in the church, what can? This is not just a Catholic problem. Students used to be the engine of the social and cultural laboratory, but now they seem to be laser-focused on their majors and minors, and the myriad extra-curricular activities (which also have a mandatory quality to them, as an expectation put on students), so that students don't have time to shake things up—not in society, even less in the church. In the late 1960s and 1970s, universities were breeding grounds for the social and ecclesial

---

[8] See Rafael Luciani and Serena Noceti, *Sinodalmente: Forma y reforma de una Iglesia sinodal* (Madrid: PPC, 2023).

movements coming to the surface.[9] However, after those years there was an ebb, a retreat. And now? Surely a number of Catholics don't feel nostalgia for those turbulent years, but even so, it is a massive change to the landscape compared to Vatican II and the early post–Vatican II period. Despite the worries about "woke" Catholics and the "campus left," there is a separation between the university and the church, but also between the church and social movements—and maybe a worrying kind of separation between Catholic universities, the church, and the outside world.

"Catholic schools remain essential places for the evangelization of the young," wrote Pope Francis on March 28, 2019, in *Christus Vivit*, the apostolic exhortation following the Synod on Young People of 2018. But this is not how the synodal process viewed them. The absence of the Catholic universities from the synodal process is the response of a lack of interest by the institutional church in the role of universities. This says a lot about the separation between the church and the youth as a movement—also because it has become hard to identify "youth" and "university students" as one movement or even as different movements.

The task should not be left to heroic individuals, faculty members, or campus ministers to try to build or rebuild the relationship with the church—a church that has no council like a Vatican III in sight, and for which synodality is the most important opportunity for an the intra-Catholic peace process (as French Jesuit theologian Christoph Theobald put it: *voie de pacification*) trying to overcome the age of culture-wars polarization.[10] The distance between Catholic university theology and the synodal process has been the symptom of a larger phenomenon: the transition of the churches to a minority situation in a context of secularization

---

[9] See, for example, *Revolte in der Kirche? Das Jahr 1968 und seine Folgen*, ed. Sebastian Holzbrecher, Julia Knop, Benedikt Kranemann, and Jörg Seiler (Freiburg: Herder, 2018).

[10] See Christoph Theobald, *Un nouveau concile qui ne dit pas son nom? Le synode sur la synodalité, voie de pacification et de créativité* (Paris: Salvator, 2023).

in the Western world, weakening the opportunity for founding theoretical models in the history of social sciences of religious (Durkheim, Weber, Troeltsch) to capture twenty-first-century dynamics.[11] The limits of the usefulness of the distinction between church and sect has taken a particular form in the context of the rise of neo-traditionalist and neo-integralist theologies within the Catholic intellectual circles in the twenty-first century.

University, Theology, and Ministerial Formation

The marginal role of Catholic colleges and universities in the synodal process has not been an exception. The current intra-Catholic conversation about the future of ministry tends to focus on new frontiers. At the official level the taboo has been broken regarding the possibility of at least discussing reform in ministry (*viri probati*, women deacons), but a key question is rethinking the contribution of academic theology to the formation of *all* those in ministry. This begins with a new awareness that the teaching and research of theology are also ecclesial ministry.

This is part of a much larger issue. The relationship between academic formation and the ecclesiastical career system is being redefined by the polycrisis (abuse and gender especially) in ways that make it more difficult to match the Tridentine system of the seminary with the needs of the church in the world today. At their fall meeting of 2019, the US bishops adopted the sixth edition of the *Program of Priestly Formation* for US dioceses and religious orders. While not a new model, it is a transitional step toward a new model.[12] In the meantime, much of the

---

[11] See Danièle Hervieu-Léger, *Le pèlerin et le converti: La religion en mouvement* (Paris: Flammarion, 1999).

[12] See *Program of Priestly Formation,* 6th ed. (Washington, DC: United States Conference of Catholic Bishops, 2022). It was developed by the USCCB Committee on Clergy, Consecrated Life, and Vocations and was promulgated on June 24, 2022.

conversation centers around the solid argument coming from various quarters of the church that seminary formation needs to be more open to the formation of lay ministers with whom they will need to cooperate as they move to an ordination process and become priests. It is not just a question of breaking the barriers between the formation of the clergy and the laity (lay ministers' formation). There is also an issue with the relationship between seminary formation and today's world of knowledge; after the Council of Trent, when the seminary for priestly formation was invented, that world of knowledge (religious and beyond) used to be housed in that ecclesiastical institution much more than today.[13] Compared to their origins, the priorities of this relationship have now been inverted. In the early centuries of its existence, after the Council of Trent, the seminary was concerned with literacy and intellectual formation and assumed that all candidates came from religious, Christian, and Catholic families within a religious culture and society. Today, seminary life focuses more on personal, psychological, and spiritual formation as set apart from the rest of the world than on making candidates to the priesthood able to handle the intellectual challenges of preaching and witnessing the gospel in a church that everywhere faces strong headwinds, where faith/religious sensibility is only one of the many options.[14]

A well-known problem today is how seminarians can get this *intellectual* formation combined with a necessary *ecclesial* dimension. There are countries where lay theologians, seminarians, and young priests in formation study together at state universities where there is a faculty of Catholic theology; seminary formation takes place in a seminary building separated from but close to the university; and that formation is about community, life of prayer,

---

[13] See Katarina Schuth, *Seminary Formation: Recent History, Current Circumstances, New Directions* (Collegeville MN: Liturgical Press, 2016).

[14] See Hans Joas, *Faith as an Option: Possible Futures for Christianity* (Stanford, CA: Stanford University Press, 2014; original German Herder 2012).

and training for pastoral ministry. This raises the issue of the role of Catholic colleges and universities especially in North America, which have some shared origins in the idea of an institution in charge of propagating theological education (as included in the formation of the clergy), but now these same Catholic higher education institutions have become the least likely places to see seminarians taking courses from their departments of theology.

What is happening to seminary formation is a challenge not only for the institutional church, but also for Catholic academia. Catholic colleges and universities can remain largely marginalized from the formation of priests, or they can try to become part of the solution in the cultural and intellectual future of the clergy. Catholic colleges and universities have a role to play, in a way that is appropriate for institutions that require a degree of autonomy and independence from the hierarchical church, and the need to protect academic freedom, while offering rigorous theological academic study and addressing social, cultural, political, and societal questions in authentic and challenging ways. The debate on the reform of the seminaries, therefore, should raise a few questions about the future of academia itself, because the crisis of the seminaries is under the spotlight in a way that the crisis of the role of Catholic academic theology is not—but should be.

If it is true that seminary formation is too cut off from the real lives of Catholics, the same could be said for academic theology, despite the visible evidence of theologians with an ecclesial intentionality who do wonderful work for the people of God. It is not a question of personal intentions, but of a cohesive, systemic position of academic theology itself within an endangered Catholic intellectual ecosystem. The institutional church needs to change its approach to formation and ministry, but academic theology requires changes as well, not solely so that future generations of Catholic clergy and lay ministers come in contact with the world of Catholic academic theology and the Catholic higher education systems, but to inform each other. It is important for academic theology to be interdisciplinary and pay attention to lived experience—including the *ecclesial* experience of who serves or are trained to serve in ordained ministry. The lack of this collaboration between university theology and seminary formation has become an argument in the hands of those who try to paint academic theology as intrinsically opposed to authentic Catholic belief.

Academic theology should *not* be taught only or primarily to advise and support the bishops and the magisterium. But the trend toward a total separation bears little hope for the future of both theology and the clergy, unless Catholic universities are intentionally defaulting into a position in which they want no role and no voice in the formation of the future generations of clergy, who in turn will contribute to the education in the faith of many of the Catholic students that keep Catholic universities going. Historically, this separation between universities and seminaries has also been a response by many theologians to those in the hierarchy who refuse to invite university theologians to contribute to seminary formation. At the same time, many of our departments of theology and religious studies have had or developed (fairly or unfairly) the reputation of communities of scholars where the reference to prayer or personal devotion was considered embarrassing and passé. So the question today is whether theology departments on Catholic campuses see themselves as having an ecclesial vocation and want to claim some responsibility or sense of duty in the formation of future lay ministers *and* clergy.[15]

The second challenge has to do with what is happening to the departments of theology and religion on the campus of Catholic colleges and universities and with what higher education itself is becoming. For a long time, universities and colleges (Catholic

---

[15] See International Theological Commission, "Theology Today: Perspectives, Principles, and Criteria," November 29, 2011.

and non-Catholic) fought to liberate themselves from the legacy of being seminaries notable for the formation of their clergy and also being run like seminaries (Catholic and non-Catholic).[16] There must be a third position between the model of mandatory chapel and the culture of displayable disengagement from the life (also the institutional life) of the church. It is not a secular model, really, but another system of faith. Now universities have become seminaries of another religion: seminaries for the formation for the high priesthood of capitalism and for the minor orders of the service economy.

This is about the viability of academic theology. There is a clear demand for core courses that attract student interest where novel approaches are given priority for hiring and tenure, but how does this interact with the ability of Catholic universities to be the locus for constructive theologizing and the transmission of the theological tradition? The need for theology courses to survive in colleges and universities where theology is still present largely due to required courses of the core curriculum has produced a fragmentation. It is not easy to "sell" theology (and not theology alone) as part of the core curriculum. The issue is now whether or not theology (along with other humanities) has a curricular rationale for being part of programs and majors that are increasingly about professional preparation. The different faiths vying for survival these days on Catholic campuses are not necessarily those mentioned in the Vatican II *Declaration on the Relation of the Church with Non-Christian Religions (Nostra Aetate)*, but rather are religious and spiritual worldviews vs. the

---

[16] See Donald G. Tewksbury, *The Founding of American Colleges and Universities before the Civil War* (New York: Teachers College, Columbia University, 1932; reprinted 1965, 2010); Richard Hofstadter and Wilson Smith, eds., *American Higher Education: A Documentary History* (Chicago: University of Chicago Press, 1961); William Smith and Thomas Bender, *American Higher Education Transformed 1940–2005: Documenting the National Discourse* (Baltimore: Johns Hopkins University Press, 2008).

"technocratic paradigm" described in Francis's *Laudato Si'*. And academic theology having failed in recent decades to teach Vatican II, including *Nostra Aetate*, is one of contributing factors to the return of different forms of anti-Judaism and anti-Semitism.

The third challenge is that the world of Catholic higher education is largely in denial about the risk of an undeclared and unacknowledged process of quiet disestablishment of theology within Catholic higher education. Catholic academics have every right and also a duty to critique, when necessary, the inadequacy of seminary formation in the Catholic Church today. But we should also be aware that academic theology operates in institutions getting rid of (or threatening to) theology requirements.

This already is affecting present and future seminarians, because before entering the seminary they have been less exposed than they used to be to theology in an academic setting; this is so even in cases where they have graduated from a Catholic college or university. Academic theologians tend to reiterate that they are not teachers of the catechism but professors of theology. This refrain made sense before "exculturation," at a time when there was a relatively solid understanding of the Catholic tradition within the students, acquired in the family, in school, and in the wider cultural environment. This understanding cannot and should no longer be presumed. The new generations of committed or militant Catholics (those who realistically will become priests and bishops) do not arrive at university as a *tabula rasa* but often having met the 24/7 online cycle of crowdsourced disinformation and propaganda about Catholicism.

Anti-Intellectualism Masked as Traditionalism

The new ecclesial landscape with which theology must live came into full display during the synodal process, which in some quarters of Anglo-American Catholicism has coincided with the return of theological anti-modernism in reactionary form, pushing against the theology elaborated by the council and developed in the post-conciliar period. This theological revanchism is not just the latest instance of an old-style institutionalist reception of Vatican II, nor is it the neo-conservative taming of the conciliar trajectories while respecting the legitimacy of Vatican II itself; rather, it has become an unapologetic indictment of Vatican II as the beginning and cause of the decline of the influence of Catholicism at the social and political level. The denigration to which conciliar theology is subjected is linked, on the neo-traditionalist side (which in the United States is *not* as sociologically and culturally marginal as in Europe), to a radical questioning of the legitimacy of the secular, pluralistic state and of liberal democracy with which Vatican II, at the end of the post-1789 "long nineteenth century," had started a process of reconciliation and dialogue.[17]

   Those who have contact with young Catholics (students and otherwise) of this generation have noticed that this revanchist movement does *not* come only by way of a few intellectuals who give simplistic answers to our uncertain times. It is part of a larger movement. The new Catholic theological anti-*aggiornamento* or anti-Vatican II agenda is part of a new search for identity that takes various forms. It sometimes begins as a particular expression of the recovery of the classical-education model;[18] sometimes takes liturgical forms (the liturgical traditionalism of the pre-conciliar Latin Mass);[19] and sometimes develops in sectarian

---

[17] See John W. O'Malley, *What Happened at Vatican II* (Cambridge, MA: Belknap Press, 2008), 53–92.

[18] See Emma Green, "Have the Liberal Arts Gone Conservative?," *New Yorker*, March 18, 2024.

[19] On the importance of liturgy in Catholic higher education, see John C. Haughey, *Where Is Knowing Going? The Horizons of the Knowing Subject* (Washington, DC: Georgetown University Press, 2009), 132: "Catholic identity, which usually is connected with morals and doctrine, needs a liturgical foundation, one that is concerned with whether God is being acknowledged as the purpose and end of the work done on campuses founded in the name of God and church."

theological-political projects.[20] The reaction against conciliar theology has become part of a theological–political imaginary that rejects liberal democracy in favor of a new neo-medieval Christianity: the church as arbiter of the political order, and the political order tasked with protecting the high sovereignty of the church. This theological–political imaginary betrays a superficial and instrumental knowledge of history. The larger issue (not only for traditionalists) is that a useful and constructive dialogue between our times and the theological and intellectual tradition of the church requires *some* expertise in the ancient world and ancient languages (especially Greek and Latin); engaging with global Catholicism today needs *someone* able to also read languages other than English. Otherwise, instead of a dialogue, it will continue to be a series of Babel-like monologues.

The resurgence of Catholic traditionalism as a reaction to the crisis of Anglo-American political-religious narratives and to the collapse of the legitimacy of Judeo-Christianity as the pillar of Western civilization has important consequences for Catholic theology. These recent trends have a direct impact on the system of intellectual production of an ecclesial and religious community that do not enjoy the shelter of the concordat system and cannot rely on a clerical system of protection (and at the same time of control) of the institutions in which theology is received, produced, and taught. The current political and economic order, in other words, exposes the church and Catholic institutions of education (but also of cultural production) to systems of political and financial patronage (with the seemingly unlimited availability of sponsors and private donors) typical of this era in the relationships between global capitalism and cultural production agencies. All this adds up to the "clash of

---

[20] For example, see the best-selling book, translated into several languages, by Rod Dreher, *The Benedict Option: A Strategy for Christians in a Post-Christian Nation* (New York: Sentinel, 2017).

civilizations" narratives that have gained new strength in light of the 2022 Russian invasion of Ukraine and the Israel-Hamas war beginning in October 2023.[21]

The politicization of ecclesial identities in the Anglo-American (now globalized) "culture wars" has led to different forms (both on the right and on the left) of anti-intellectualism, in a misappropriation of the prophetic genre and language.[22] This animus against theological liberalism has often become a revolt against theological thought as such. It is a new form of Catholic anti-intellectualism: the collapse of high culture and popular culture are fueled by the new media and social media (in some countries more than others) in which popular online preachers, proudly not belonging to academia, are redefining the relationship between knowledge and one of the most important producers of it in Western history, the Catholic Church. Some prominent Catholic voices have become detached from the church's past, one they often invoke as opposed to the present, the heralds of deep suspicion of intellectual complexity. Now the university is just one of the platforms, and much less influential, more selective, more regulated, censored and self-censored than platforms like Facebook, Instagram, Twitter (X), TikTok, and YouTube. There the new oracles operate, endowed with a kind of infallibility much more usable than papal infallibility.

If there is a consonance between the Catholic imagination and the idea of the "virtual,"[23] academic theology is institution-ally disconnected from that world, independent from the social-media visibility of individual faculty members or the branding

---

[21] For example, see former militant atheist and now high-profile convert Ayaan Hirsi Ali, "Why I Am Now a Christian: Atheism Can't Equip Us for Civilisational War," unherd.com, November 11, 2023.

[22] See Cathleen Kaveny, *Prophecy without Contempt: Religious Discourse in the Public Square* (Cambridge, MA: Harvard University Press, 2018).

[23] See Katherine G. Schmidt, *Virtual Communion: Theology of the Internet and the Catholic Sacramental Imagination* (Lanham, MD: Lexington Books/Fortress Academic, 2020).

efforts of the universities.[24] In some countries, including self-described democracies, there is also the modern version of the same old struggle between the powerful and those who dissent. In the digital age the powerful are aided by government-aligned media and/or (sometimes Catholic) media outlets funded by wealthy donors, with their online smear campaigns and troll armies.

This has also modified the relationship between universities and faculty, including theological faculty members; branding encourages professors to be active and visible in the media and social media for the sake of academic marketing, a sideshow of a disturbing trend of ecclesial marketing of specific brands of Catholicism.[25] On top of the old concerns for the protection of academic freedom from the interference of the church's hierarchies, there are now new concerns for the role of other mechanisms of censorship and self-censorship. Non-academic, anti-intellectual merchants of a simplistic approach to faith—influencers castigating the political correctness, the liberalism, the trigger warnings, the smug elites—operate from platforms and in a different space that enjoys more freedom from both the church and the new systems of knowledge production, and at the same time conceals more subtle systems of controlling culture and learning.

Catholic Universities, Sectarianism, and the Catholic Ecclesial Community

Historically, many Catholic colleges and universities in various countries were created by a church that was excluded by the

---

[24] On the branding of universities, see Kevin Ahern, "Charism, Crisis, and Adaptation: A Theological Reading of Identity in Catholic Higher Education," *Journal of Catholic Higher Education* 40, no. 2 (2021): 111–27.

[25] In what Anthony Godzieba called the "old certainties": "the juridical policing of grace, the drawing of boundaries, the branding of Catholicism." See Anthony J. Godzieba, "The Anti-Incarnational Affect and Its Overcoming," in *American Catholicism in the Twenty-First Century,* ed. Benjamin T. Peters and Nicholas Rademacher, *The Annual Publication of the College Theology Society*, vol. 63 (Maryknoll, NY: Orbis Books, 2018), 80–87.

mainstream (the Protestant mainstream in the nineteenth-century United States), with the goal of including and promoting the education and success of recent Catholic immigrants. But in the contemporary moment, universities more resemble exclusive clubs than religious communities. Also thanks to the "theology of the laity" that after Vatican II democratized theology, lay men and lay women now constitute a large part of those who teach theology. But the false egalitarianism of technocracy and meritocracy today sends the message that the liberal arts and theology are only for those rich in financial or social capital.

This is obviously a problem, especially for Catholic colleges and universities, part of a religious tradition that has made "inclusion" one of the marks of its synodal conversion as well as of its commitment to social justice that is anti-sectarian by definition.[26] Inclusion has become a theologically and doctrinally integral part of the self-understanding of the synodal church, but in higher education it is often made impossible for financial reasons, not for the historically religious or theological reasons, as before. And it is undeniable that a certain number of Catholics who care about the church (not just the bishops) perceive colleges and universities as sectarian enclaves that see themselves separated from and superior to the church, unwilling to build bridges across the theological divides. This is problematic for institutions that depend also on an ecclesial constituency and support, as far removed and mediated as we want.

For many students, college is the most concrete instance of community they have ever experienced. This is true for faculty members too. But what has been called the "country-clubization" of American universities[27] does not spare many Catholic

---

[26] See Ernst Troeltsch, *The Social Teaching of the Christian Churches*, vol. 1, trans. Olive Wyon (New York: Macmillan Company, 1931), esp. 331–43.

[27] Richard K. Vedder, quoted in Sam Dillon, "Share of College Spending for Recreation Is Rising," *New York Times*, July 9, 2010. Vedder is a professor at Ohio University who studies the economics of higher education.

institutions of higher education, especially the leading ones. This is an educational and pedagogical problem, quite visible for those who look at the schedule of an average college student today:

> How students choose to spend their leisure time shapes and changes them just as much as what they choose to do for work. Outside of the classroom, cocurricular planning must break out of the 'involvement culture' where clubs and activities have become training camps for students' resumé enhancement.[28]

From a theological and religious point of view, this presents us also with an ecclesiological problem because of the community-eroding effects of modern universities—including the risk of erosion of ecclesial communities. At the local level, every college and university is a history to itself, but the question can be posed more clearly in terms of the relationship among different brands of Catholic higher education and the construction, maintenance, or reform of a shared *sensus ecclesiae*. The problem is not just the disappearance of ecclesiology of the canon of courses offered in systematic theology. The problem is also the implicit ecclesiology of working or studying in a Catholic college or university today. All those with some connection to the world of colleges and universities today cannot help but see the academic nomadism imposed by the market forces of higher education. To some extent this is inevitable (and it was experienced centuries ago in Christendom's Europe as well). But it becomes fatal when even teaching theology is an enterprise in the hands of faculty who more and more function as independent contractors, without a sense of common mission. Except for the contact with students,

---

[28] Anna Bonta Moreland and Mark Shiffman, "Educating for What? Liberal Arts in a Professional World," in *Catholic Higher Education and Catholic Social Thought*, ed. Bernard G. Prusak and Jennifer Reed-Bouley, 99–125 (Mahwah, NJ: Paulist Press, 2023), 118.

today's academic work—with all its undeniable privileges for those who are tenured—is often a picture of monads rather than community, or in some cases, of a sense of community more focused on colleagues in national and international networks than a connection to local colleagues and students.

This isolation has a deep effect on the work and vocation of theologians. And except for classroom time with the students (if the class is not online), it is also an isolation from students and (for those who are Catholic) from their lived Catholicism.[29] *Universitas* and *humanitas* now do not seem bound to meet on our campuses, and the isolation of the theologian is part of this situation: "The much more general experience of loneliness is so contradictory to the human condition of plurality that it is simply unbearable for any length of time and needs the company of God, the only imaginable witness of good works if it is not to annihilate human existence altogether."[30] Far from the spiritual experience of solitude, today's loneliness of theologians comes also from the fact that their authority used to be guaranteed by the authority of the church and by the promise that learning was the recipe for success in the future—both elements of the equation now largely unknown.

The spatial location of Catholic colleges and universities and the mutual relationship among them represent even visually what the French sociologist Jérôme Fourquet called the "archipelisation" of society. This fragmentation into an archipelago applies also to the Catholic Church.[31] But on college campuses today

---

[29] Paul Lakeland, "The Habit of Empathy: Postmodernity and the Future of the Church-Related College," in *Professing in the Postmodern Academy: Faculty and the Future of Church-Related Colleges*, ed. Stephen R. Haynes (Waco, TX: Baylor University Press, 2005), 533–48.

[30] Hannah Arendt, *The Human Condition* (Chicago: University of Chicago Press, 1958), 76.

[31] See Jérôme Fourquet, *L'archipel français: Naissance d'une nation multiple et divisée* (Paris: Seuil, 2019).

the end of the sense that faculty (especially theology faculty) do something visibly *together*, as a collective and as a communal act, reflects the acceptance of a neo-liberal model of work that has no interest in the social connections—and even less in the ecclesial bonds of communion. The lack of time for contemplative interactions among faculty, among students, and among faculty and students is not a bug but a feature of today's campus life; there is a compulsion of activity and "a compulsion of communication [that] leads to the reproduction of the same, to conformism. . . . 'Repressive forces don't stop people expressing themselves but rather force them to express themselves.'"[32] This compulsion to communicate reinforces sectarian instincts.

This is not just a spiritual or ecclesiological or ecclesial concern; it also has consequences on the future of the profession. The church (not the hierarchical church, but the notion of *ekklesia* as a community) is one of the last resorts against de-territorialization and de-localization of knowledge and its sources. It is hard to imagine a Catholic resistance to the corporatized college if even theologians (but more generally, in a different way, the faculty in Catholic colleges and universities) stay detached from the local church and its sacramentally rooted localization.

The call to a conversion of the theological profession in Catholic colleges and universities comes at a critical time—the polycrisis of sexism, racism, and sexual abuse in the church. Once the problem of theology was how to relate with the marginal role of intellectual life in American Catholicism: the backwardness of American Catholic higher education, the anti-intellectualism of Americans in general, the persistence of anti-Catholic bigotry in the United States, and the long-standing need of the American bishops to devote their limited financial

---

[32] Byung-Chul Han, *Vita Contemplativa: In Praise of Inactivity*, trans. Daniel Steuer (Polity Press, 2024); *Vita contemplativa: Oder von der Untätigkeit* (Berlin: Bullstein, 2022), 18. The quotation is from Gilles Deleuze, "Mediators," in *Negotiations 1972–1990* (New York: Columbia University Press, 1995), 129.

resources to the basic literacy and elementary-level education of poor immigrants.[33] But we are now in a new phase. The process of de-theologization and the lack of intellectual vocations is not just the result of different career choices by young Catholics but is also part of the refusal to become morally co-responsible with a church identified (and not just by the media, but also by part of the theological establishment) with sexism, racism, and sexual abuse. The past of the church (both distant and recent) is on the stand as a defendant, and the future is already a prime suspect, a possible criminal in the making. And on the stand of the defendants, there is symbolically also academic theology.

There is a problem of preservation and defense of the *idea* of the theological and intellectual tradition against anti-intellectualism. But we should be careful not to turn ourselves into what Hannah Arendt called the "professional preservers."[34] Denying that sexism, racism, and the sex-abuse crisis affect our relationship with Vatican II would signal a dangerous imperviousness to the signs of our times. The polycrisis of sexism, racism, and sexual abuse poses serious questions to the doctrinal order set by Vatican II, but it also challenges the reformulation of the relations between church and university, as well as the role of the church in culture, society, and the education system.

The post–Vatican II church had inculturation on the agenda. Today, the Catholic cultural and education system is not exempt from what Olivier Roy called "the erasement of the implicit," the weakening of the nonexplicit forms of transmission of values and

---

[33] See John Tracy Ellis, "American Catholics and the Intellectual Life," *Thought* 30 (Autumn 1955). Ellis was professor of church history at Catholic University of America in Washington, DC, and managing editor of *The Catholic Historical Review*.

[34] See Hannah Arendt, *Men in Dark Times* (Harcourt, Brace, and World, 1968), 193.

norms that has taken the form of a "de-culturation,"[35] and not just of what Danièle Hervieu-Léger identified in the early 2000s as "exculturation."[36] Even in historically Catholic countries, Catholic culture has become a subculture that does not need to think of itself within the framework of a dominant culture; individuals see themselves as members of a minority within the larger society, but also within their own church.

This requires a different kind of relationship between university and the church, one that cannot be afraid to put together critical inquiry exercised in academic freedom and call to discipleship. As Anthony Godzieba put it a few years ago:

> This is the contemporary situation in which Christian discipleship is embedded, at least where consumer capitalism and its technologies prevail. Various forms of contemporary Catholic dogmatism—or, better put, attempts to reduce Catholic identity to a single identity-marker or a "brand"—are capitulations to this inertia, even while claiming to resist the social changes that provoke it. In other words, attempts to "trademark" Catholicism as "settled doctrine" or an ethereal metaphysical realm, or to reduce it to strictly literal readings of Vatican II texts or the Catechism, or to conflate it with Catholic social thought or inflexible liturgical law are anxiety-prone reactions to the accelerated speed of social change and overwhelming difference. They are also ways of minimizing the lived performance of discipleship and the basic need for these applicative moments to play out over time in order to clarify their meaning. . . . If there is to be any critique of contemporary culture by

---

[35] See Olivier Roy, *L'aplatissement du monde: La crise de la culture et l'empire des normes* (Paris: Seuil, 2022), 49–69.

[36] About the concept of exculturation, see Danièle Hervieu-Léger, *Catholicisme, la fin d'un monde* (Paris: Bayard, 2003).

Catholic theology (I refuse to use the term "culture war"), the issue is not liberal-vs.-conservative, pre-Vatican-II-vs.-post-Vatican-II, traditionalist-vs.-progressive. The real point is to critique the eclipse of time and narrative that affects our experience of discipleship, and the temptation to de-temporalize Christian faith in reaction to what the theologian David Ford has called the "multiple overwhelm-ings" of the present.[37]

The present has become overwhelming and led us into "presentism."[38] Theologians were once trained to think like historians—even Catholic theologians, despite the proverbial suspicion of the institutional church against historians.[39] Now they are trained to think more like politicians or social workers—where every theology has become or is supposed to be a form of socially engaged political theology. This has effectively "de-ecclesialized" the work of theologians and has de-theologized the ecclesial conversation both *ad intra* and *ad extra*. While trying to make theology less "churchy" and more current, this de-eccle-sialization and de-theologization have opened spaces for forces that are not less problematic than the old clericalist monopoly on the knowledge of the church. The gradual diminishment

---

[37] Anthony J. Godzieba, "'. . . And Followed Him on the Way' (Mark 10:52): Unity, Diversity, Discipleship," in *Beyond Dogmatism and Innocence: Hermeneutics, Critique, and Catholic Theology,* ed. Anthony J. Godzieba and Bradford E. Hinze, 228–54 (Collegeville, MN: Liturgical Press, 2017). The reference is to David Ford, *Theology: A Very Short Introduction* (Oxford/New York: Oxford University Press, 1999), 7–11.

[38] See François Hartog, *Régimes d'historicité: Présentisme et expériences du temps* (Paris: Seuil, 2003). In English, *Regimes of Historicity: Presentism and Experiences of Time* (New York: Columbia University Press, 2015).

[39] I want to thank here Kathryn Lofton (Yale University) for the insights in the lecture delivered at Villanova University on October 4, 2023, titled "Why History Is the Battlefield: What the Study of Religion Teaches."

and obsolescence of *theological and ecclesial* discourse within the
university will only make it more likely that in coming generations that space could be ceded entirely to the YouTube hacks
and reactionary traditionalists who happily grift on people's
(including students') existential questions in an impoverished
version of old-style apologetics.[40]

This is where the controversies about teaching on race, gender, and sexuality exemplify the challenge before us; among
them, accepting the fact that some parts of the doctrinal and
magisterial tradition of the church have already been liquidated
(for example, by Vatican II on anti-Judaism)—a precedent that
cannot be sanitized and isolated as exceptional and unique. But
any realistic and sustainable path toward doctrinal development
must reject the prospects of a dissolution of the tradition.[41]
Doctrinal development has to happen in a porosity anchored in
God—a porosity that leaves behind hierarchical self-referentiality,
but also is anchored in a way that avoids consumerism and the
production mindset hijacked by trendiness and the intellectual
fashions of the moment.

If theologians focus on ethnography, cultural studies, and ac-
tivist political theology, leaving behind the dogmatics, patristics,
ecclesiology, philosophical and fundamental theology, eventually
the vacuum is going to be filled by the self-appointed "watch-
dogs" policing grace in this new quest for a kind of ultra-vigilant
Catholic pride. Complaint against the church has become central
to the self-definition of the identity of a number of Catholics
in ways essentially different from the age of "dissent" in the
post–Vatican II period. The newly self-directed, ethnographical,

---

[40] This problem was identified by Gaillardetz even before the appearance of
social media and the rise of Catholic influencers. See Richard R. Gaillardetz,
"Do We Need a New(er) Apologetics?" *America*, February 2, 2004.

[41] See Anne M. Carpenter, *Nothing Gained Is Eternal: A Theology of Tradition*
(Minneapolis: Fortress Press, 2022).

and political aren't equivalent to or automatically theological and ecclesial.[42]

On the other side, some theologians hold a naive fascination with Silicon-Valley-fueled futurism that refuses to acknowledge the limits of technology within social goals or structures.[43] This approach to tradition and the future translates into an "unmooring from history, that is, like telling history 'step aside because I'm not interested,'" a sign of "no respect for the patience of God's steps in history."[44] Unless Catholic theologians come to recognize that constant critical contextual analysis cannot alone satisfy our existential hunger, we will see philosophical speculative theology become the terrain of bad actors—not only intellectually, but also pastorally, as the teaching of theology holds within it a seriousness in the care of students in the totality of their humanity.

This unmooring risks a disembodied and de-materialized theological scholarship. For all its anthropological fascination with the material objects of religion, theology today cannot become mute and paralyzed vis-à-vis the lived religion of the real church, with a special view to our students. Theological thought is integrative and by its wholistic nature not possible without the dimension of personal experience that is also shared experience.

---

[42] See important reflections on the relationship between the private/intimate and the public/political (but also, by extension, the ecclesial) in the works of Lauren Berlant (1957–2021), including *Cruel Optimism* (Durham, NC: Duke University Press, 2011).

[43] About the turn since the mid 2010s from Silicon Valley's culture of technological optimism to post-rational, neo-pagan openness to the religious, the numinous, and the spiritualities of "popular neo-Jungianism" (for example, Jordan Peterson, closely connected with bishop Robert Barron), see Tara Isabella Burton, "Rational Magic: Why a Silicon Valley Culture That Was Once Obsessed with Reason Is Going Woo," *The New Atlantis*, Spring 2023.

[44] Italo Mancini, *Tornino i volti* (Genova: Marietti, 1989), 34, 35, my translation.

Academic Theology and the Sex-Abuse Crisis

There is no addressing academic theology today without the felt weight of the sex-abuse crisis, which deeply affects how students study theology and how we do research and teach theology. Since 2019, I have taught an undergraduate course on the sex-abuse crisis in the Catholic Church, and this course has been the most intense—emotionally, psychologically, but also theologically—teaching experience of my life in the classroom. But the course is also an illuminating experience as I witness what the students have to say in class and have written about in their papers. If there is one thing I've learned from this course, it's that Catholic universities need to engage with this new generation of Catholics, who have grown up surrounded by news articles on the crisis. As one student said in class: "The church of the sex-abuse scandal is the only church we know." Another student and recent convert said at a conference: "Converting to the Catholic Church—it's converting also to the sex-abuse crisis."

Currently, there is an internal battle in Catholicism over the root causes of the sexual-abuse crisis. Some believe it has to do with the institutional framework itself, as well as the theological aspects of the Catholic Church, which have led to the abuse as well as long-lasting impacts on victims. Others, however, believe that the sexual revolution and Vatican II have caused the sexual-abuse crisis. Far deeper than the usual theological fault lines, since 2017, dealing with the sex-abuse crisis in the Catholic Church has become inseparable from the larger MeToo movement and the discourse on gender and identity. The generation of students currently attending Catholic universities is in the middle of this debate. All this happens in the context of, and contributes to, the separation between academic theology and the church.

The modern history of the sexual-abuse crisis in the Catholic Church has solidified a certain ecclesiological narrative; it is a systemic crisis caused by abusive members of the church (not just priests) and by a catastrophic failure of the episcopal hierarchy in dealing with them. The problem is that this is only partially true. Unpopular as it may be to say this in my own field, there were and are other failures in the Catholic Church in responding to the phenomenon. Among those failures are how the intellectual and academic sectors—including theologians—have failed to robustly bring academic thought and theological weight to challenge, inform, and provide historical context where episcopal hierarchy and theology have not only faltered, but failed to address the seriousness, the devastation, of this crisis.

This crisis the Catholic Church has been going through in the last few decades has produced the spectacular fall from grace of cardinals, bishops, and entire episcopates in various countries. We have our gaze on the hierarchy, and rightly so. But few are looking at the role of pontifical and/or Catholic universities, departments of theology and/or religious studies in Catholic universities and academies in addressing the crisis.

Yes, Catholic universities have launched a series of initiatives, mostly in the form of public debates and high-profile lectures. However, this approach supplements and is a consequence of the journalistic work on the sex-abuse crisis; it is not a direct address to the crisis that academic theology has the means to bring forth. The public debates and lectures cannot substitute for the role theology must play at this moment. Public panels with high-profile speakers will not by themselves be able to change the terms of the conversation or add ongoing meaningful intellectual contribution to it, which is something that universities have the means to do and that they must provide. But to this point no major center or institute has been created in a Catholic university (at least in the United States) to research, study, and address the very different aspects of the sex-abuse crisis and its effects on the church and rippling through *all* theological disciplines: scripture and tradition, history, liturgy, ecclesiology, sacraments, and soteriology. No aspect of theology has been untouched, and academic theology uniquely has a profound role to play.

This is not to say that theologians have not sought to address this situation. There is abundant and fine literature available on the sex-abuse crisis. But the crisis is also a spiritual crisis, and the engagement of academia cannot be based merely on short-term, well-funded, three-year or five-year projects, after which programs move on to something else. The fact is that in the Catholic Church there has been so far no systemic, organized effort by Catholic theologians to think about and find ways to address the sexual-abuse crisis. What became public, especially after the 2002 *Boston Globe* investigative reports and the new phase that started in 2018, could and should have sparked a vast theological rethinking as new approaches, new resources and understandings became available to tackle key intellectual issues for the life of the church.[45] Take an earlier example of how academic tradition addressed a different aspect of the church. After the opening, in 1998, of the Archives of the Holy Office and the Congregation of the Index of Forbidden Books, a series of studies were launched by important universities with collections of monographs and dictionaries providing authoritative, scholarly answers.

At more than twenty years after the *Boston Globe* investigation, there has been no cohesive, coordinated, large-scale address of a major concern of both the church and academic theology, even as Catholic theologians say the sex-abuse crisis represents an existential challenge in the life of the church. Yet, acknowledging the crisis and seeing how academic theology might offer insights,

---

[45] See Massimo Faggioli and Mary Catherine O'Reilly-Gindhart, "A New Wave in the Modern History of the Abuse Crisis in the Catholic Church: Literature Overview, 2018–2020," *Theological Studies* 82, no. 1 (March 2021): 156–85.

study, and resources for this moment, one has to admit that not much has changed in the institutional approach to the profession of being an academic theologian.

This is not due to lack of awareness or a failure to be willing to act by individual scholars; rather, it is part of an institutional development typical of the post–Vatican II period that hinders the larger role of theology. The tensions between the magisterium and theologians beginning with the dissent around *Humanae Vitae* in 1968 produced a mutual alienation between hierarchy and theologians, and on the part of theologians, reasonable fears for their academic freedom. This is the paradigm in which academic theology still operates. How the sex-abuse crisis has not yet been the seismic shock to the Catholic Church to seek the work, study, and insight of the theological academics is a question that has not yet pierced or changed the paradigm of mutual fear and power structures.

Academic theology is facing several pressures: from the church, from Catholic colleges and universities, and most of all from market forces in higher education. Given how the evaluation system of faculty works, it is understandable that young theologians are reluctant to engage in a field of research like the Catholic sex-abuse crisis, a minefield for reasons that span from the methodological (relationship between scholarship and activism) to the political (both church politics and secular politics) to the financial (the embarrassment of Catholic donors and alumni at the idea of funding an institute or a center dedicated to the study of sexual abuse in the church). What is less comprehensible is that established Catholic theologians and administrators of Catholic institutions of higher education have not considered it an institutional and scholarly priority to support research on the sex-abuse crisis at the institutional level. As one of the leading experts on safeguarding and prevention of sexual abuse, Jesuit theologian and psychologist Hans Zollner writes:

What one finds, however, is that even in the academic world there is still little real sign of an awareness of or readiness for a long-term commitment. There can be no other explanation for the fact that not even in theology faculties around the world has an engagement with the specific theological questions raised by the sex-abuse crisis led to a long-term interest that goes beyond individual initiatives.[46]

The sex-abuse crisis has revealed a tragic vacuum in the understanding of the church about this phenomenon, its causes, and consequences. Nature abhors a vacuum, and this vacuum is now being filled and outsourced to news media, journalism, and the criminal justice system. The gap between journalism and church tradition is wider than the gap between the tradition of the church and its history. It simply is not possible to offer a theological evaluation of a crisis in the tradition of the church without doing the historiographical work on its context. The church dealing with the sex-abuse scandal needs more than the "rough draft of history" provided by news journalism.

Work has been done on the sex-abuse crisis in other fields, including church history, but if Catholic scholars continue to address this crisis as individual scholars and only in the context of the overspecialization in academia, which keeps researchers and students from seeing the larger context of the scientific problems they face, those scholars will have little impact on the understanding of the crisis in global Catholicism.

We are in the biggest crisis in the life of the church in the post–Vatican II period, possibly since the Reformation and/or precipitating another Reformation. And Catholic theology needs

---

[46] Hans Zollner, SJ, "What Does It Mean to Come to Terms with Abuse? Some Suggestions," in *Abuse in the Church,* ed. Michelle Becka, Po-Ho Huang, and Gianluca Montaldi, *Concilium* 4, 119–27 (2023), 125.

to be called on to engage in a wave of long-term, coordinated, and systematic research projects helping the church face the sexual-abuse crisis in order to prepare tools for the thinking of the church; not just for the sake of prevention, but also for helping the church sum up the courage to correct the theological errors that contributed to the sexual abuses. Given the global history and geography of the sex-abuse crisis, Catholic universities have a special and unique role to play—and not just for the church but also for other institutions and religious traditions recently beginning to deal with the phenomenon.

If Catholic institutions of education limit themselves to developing and implementing good practices and safe-space policies on campus, they abandon the field to the different forces trying to take advantage of the sex-abuse crisis for specific, political, and idiosyncratic agendas.

5

Catholic Theology vis-à-vis *Ecclesia, Universitas,* and *Civitas*

Academic Freedom, from Christendom to Diaspora

The current ecclesial situation has seen the return of liturgical traditionalism, anti-scientific sentiment (even anti-intellectualism), and a persistent media climate focusing on multiple scandals in the Catholic Church. At the same time, academic theology has been part of a marginalization not only by the culture industry but by universities as well—a situation that isn't new, but growing more overt. Historically speaking, the church hierarchy's indifference and at times hostility to academic theology is not new either. But this time it is not coming only from clericalist and traditionalist circles. Anti-intellectualism has become one of the markers of the "culture" of Catholicism today, in which an emphasis on the pastoral is used in opposition to the doctrinal (of the teachings of Vatican II), but also as a repudiation of the supposed elitism of the academic world.

This is not just an opportunistic riding of the spirit of the times, but also a response to the shift in theological scholarship toward a horizon that is not just post-institutional but also post-ecclesial, which implies an almost complete functional and existential separation from ecclesiastical authority and the people of God. This separation has brought more independence from the church, while not necessarily greater authority, freedom, or creativity to Catholic theology and to the Catholic intellectual conversation. Instead, this separation has created new and more subtle dependencies. The disconnection between academic theology and the ecclesial intellectual ecosystem has deprived theology of an essential reference precisely at a time when vast social and cultural changes urgently require a connection to the ecclesial system, which offers and requires a conversion, including for theological thinking.[1]

This conversion is necessary because the conquest of academic freedom, by a mostly lay-led Catholic theology and helped by enlightened leaders of Catholic higher education, took place in the post–Vatican II period, in an ecclesial and institutional order within Christendom enjoying the last fruits of its legacy. Now we are much closer, not just in Europe but also in other areas of the West, to a situation of diaspora. It is the diaspora of Christianity in the world between the secular and the post-secular, but it is also the diaspora of "religion" in the university today. As Christoph Theobald notes:

> It is not uncommon for our theological faculties—as indeed the university more generally—to offer the students "a fragmented and often disintegrated panorama of contemporary university studies" (*Veritatis Gaudium*, 4c), putting before them the same lack of transparency and the same differentiation of internal aspects of the areas that theology encounters in contemporary society. Hence the spiritual challenge of leading theology toward a perception of the Christian

---

[1] On the need to reintegrate the place of contemplative vision in our view of the *polis*, see Byung-Chul Han, *Vita Contemplativa: In Praise of Inactivity*. trans. Daniel Steuer (Medford, MA: Polity, 2024), 62–64.

tradition that is both complex and unified; a challenge that is more largely that of our entire post-modern civilization scarred by the perverse effects of extreme differentiation of cultural spheres or fields of existence, threatened by the resulting violence and confronted all the more strongly with the desire for unity of subjects, groups and societies.[2]

A diasporic situation should lead theology to taking a different approach, not just to being enfolded by a post-Christendom world, university, and church. Unless it abandons a gladiatorial role, in constant and semi-automatic takedown of the teaching of the church, theology will experience more humiliation rather than humility.[3] Without that conversion, academic theology will continue to serve, but have a much smaller audience, even as it becomes more self-referential, superfluous, and isolated—not just from the church, but from the rest of academia and the public square.

But a conversion like this requires a change of high policies and priorities coming from administrators. Given the vital role that universities play in our knowledge-based and faith-based (also faith in the market, in sciences) societies, Catholic institutions of higher education should not be understood as private but rather as public institutions. This is in line with the Catholic understanding of working for the common good and also relevant to understanding the role of theology in Catholic universities, where administrators have a responsibility—civil, public, and ecclesial—not just to one particular constituency but to a wider one.

---

[2] Christoph Theobald, "Faire de la théologie au service d'un christianisme en diaspora: Pour un pragmatisme éclairé," in *Faire de la théologie dans un christianisme diasporique,* special issue of *Recherches de Science Religieuse* 107, no. 3 (2019): 515 (translation mine).

[3] See Zena Hitz, *Lost in Thought: The Hidden Pleasures of an Intellectual Life* (Princeton, NJ: Princeton University Press, 2020), 9.

Theology in the Wider Society, the Academy, and the Church: Relationships under Review

More than forty years ago, David Tracy gave theology "three distinct and related social realities [with which to interact]: the wider society, the academy, and the church."[4] Currently we are witnessing a scenario where theology meets with a marginalization from all three of these spheres, although the presence of theology in Catholic higher education remains (at least in the United States) more visible than in the other two spheres. But this is already changing.

Catholic higher education plays a key role in the global church. The Western model of the university is still a guide and a model for the Western world. Catholic universities have adopted that role and accepted a model of relationships between knowledge and the economic system in the system of advanced global capitalism. In the West it is a world of private, non-state institutions in which knowledge and scholarship are fully inserted into the market system of advanced capitalism—as seen in the need to recruit students who pay very high university fees, but also in the need to fit in and pressure to conform to a cultural mainstream that limits the freedom of research and the teaching of theology (even in the face of an almost total freedom in regard to ecclesiastical institutions).

Catholic academic institutions in the United States benefit from support from the government at national and state levels in ways that are minimal or marginal compared to the Catholic universities in European countries. For that reason US Catholic universities compete for funding with secular and public academic institutions, as well as other religious schools. Catholic universities are also in competition with one another, enjoying a high

---

[4] David Tracy, *The Analogical Imagination: Christian Theology and the Culture of Pluralism* (New York: Crossroad, 1981), 5.

degree of independence from ecclesiastical authority (the bishops, the Vatican) even as they are governed by boards (councils) comprised of large donors, lawyers, and entrepreneurs—making it difficult to distinguish them from non-Catholic universities in structure, approach, and spirit.

What keeps Catholic universities and theology departments, courses, and programs alive is also an ecclesial ecosystem now on the path to change, reform, and transformation; this is one of the roots of the identity and mission crisis. It's not just a US-based Judeo-Christian national theological-political narrative under review, but a nineteenth and twentieth centuries *national* theological-political narrative of European and Western countries.[5] As the Catholic Church also is reexamining its relationship with theology and theologians, a consequence of the globalization and de-Occidentalization of Catholicism, it insinuates the idea that the humanities and liberal arts, in their latest iterations—postcolonial and cultural studies—are a symptom of cultural and spiritual decadence, in opposition to "true" theology.

The Anglophone scene within which theology is usually placed is that of the so-called culture wars—progressive liberalism versus social conservatism, a fracture that aligns with that of the two-party political system in the United States. But however pervasive the culture wars are in this day, these narrative risks offer facile relief to those who find themselves in ideologically opposed camps of villain or scapegoat within the marginalization of religious knowledge and theology. In the North American academic world after Vatican II, Catholic universities were faced with the need to compete with their Protestant as well as secular counterparts at the academic level (research) and in relation to academic freedom apart from religious authorities. The solutions given by the administrators of Catholic universities in

---

[5] See Anthony Pagden, *Oltre gli Stati: Poteri, popoli e ordine globale* (Bologna: Il Mulino, 2023).

the wake of the 1967 "Land O' Lakes Statement" were mod-
eled after mainstream university education on the national and
international levels; their identity could be defined as liberal-
progressive, where business schools and the "hard sciences" held
the center. While academic theology met the challenge, winning
on both fronts (academic excellence and academic freedom), it
was where it intersected with a series of intra-ecclesial battles
and in particular in reaction to John Paul II's *Ex Corde Ecclesiae*
of 1990, seeing it as a unilateral imposition of a certain type of
Catholicism and an idea of Catholic education against its new-
found freedoms.[6]

Three decades after *Ex Corde Ecclesiae*, the existential crisis
of many Catholic universities was deepened by their attempt to
distance themselves from the specific mission of education of a
Catholic tradition in which theology had a strong emphasis on
the human sciences and on human and cultural education in the
broadest sense. In recent years in the world of Catholic colleges
and universities that skew liberal-progressive there has been a
tendency to redefine the Catholic identity and the mission of the
university with phrases such as "in the Catholic tradition," which
tend to be interpreted in very different ways, but almost always
lead to a reduction in the number of theology courses required of
all students and therefore to a reduction in the consistency and role
(or in some cases to the disappearance) of theology departments.

But Catholic theology in our universities is still largely blind
to this situation. The fear of a return of tyranny on the part of
the ecclesiastical authorities is still stronger—a fear reflex—than
the fear of being at the mercy of those who dominate Catholic

---

[6] For a critique of the American reception of *Ex Corde Ecclesiae,* see
Stephen M. Hildebrand and Sean Sheridan, *Fidelity and Freedom:* Ex Corde
Ecclesiae *at Twenty-Five* (Steubenville, OH: Franciscan University Press; Balti-
more, MD: The Catholic University of America Press 2018). See also *Institu-
tional Principles for Catholic Identity and Mission Assessment: A Best Practices Guide*
(Washington, DC: Association of Catholic Colleges and Universities, 2018).

institutions, those lay managers and technocrats often barely familiar with Catholicism. This has disruptive effects on the position of Catholic theology in the academic world and its credibility, as it has become compromised with a de-culturation, which is a form of silencing in disguise and contradicts the proclamation of diversity, equity, and inclusion (DEI).

One solution to the problematic relationship between the Catholic tradition and DEI is affirming that in the church no one "owns" the tradition (however it is defined) and that the tradition perfectly mirrors nobody. This means *not* buying into identity politics. Although substantially different in key ways, scholars of classics and scholars of the Christian tradition and theology face similar challenges today related to conversations around colonialism, whiteness, slavery, gender, and patriarchy. As Mary Beard puts it:

> The overall strength of Classics is not to be measured by exactly how many young people know Latin and Greek from school or university. It is better measured by asking how many believe that there should be people in the world who do know Latin and Greek, how many people think that there is an expertise in that worth taking seriously—and ultimately paying for.[7]

But there is also another solution beyond the temptation merely to revive theology as part of identity politics, and that

---

[7] Mary Beard, *Confronting the Classics: Traditions, Adventures, and Innovations* (New York: Norton, 2013), 13. Some of the reflections on our relationship with the past, developed by Beard in her May 2019 series of Gifford Lectures at the University of Edinburgh, "The Ancient World and Us: From Fear and Loathing to Enlightenment and Ethics" (which included lecture titles "Murderous Games," "Whiteness," "Lucretia and the Politics of Sexual Violence," "Them and Us," "Tyranny and Empire," and "Classical Civilization?"), continue to be pertinent for Catholic theologians as well.

is a solution concerned with the intrinsic value of Christian or Catholic theology. What is its intrinsic value if it is not rooted somehow to the ongoing development of the life of the church as a community of disciples attempting to live Jesus-like lives? The importance of personal spiritual development as a goal of theological education, if seen as limited, individualized, and separate from church, is a secondary and even derivative goal. And the so-called liberal arts skills that theology and religious-studies departments try to portray as helpful for getting a job (critical thinking and workplace "soft skills") are really tertiary goals.[8]

Catholic Theology and Post-Institutionalism

It is important to see the situation of theology in higher education today within the larger crisis of the role of universities and the nineteenth-century German model of university, compared to the rise of other centers of knowledge and scholarship today. Theology must deal not only with the power of the technocratic paradigm over theology, humanities, and the liberal arts, but also with the decline of universities in favor of other types of research centers.[9]

This includes the influence of the think-tank model, which shapes the idea of university as harbored by private donors (whose interests in knowledge combine with their interest in politics and the economic system). Alongside this influence, there is also competition from new institutions that rely on distance-learning courses, removing students from in-person learning. Often this type of learning disembodies the relationship between

---

[8] For important considerations on the intrinsic value of the humanities and liberal arts, see Christopher Newfield, "Criticism after This Crisis: Toward a National Strategy for Literary and Cultural Study," *Representations* 164, no. 1 (November 2023): 1–22.

[9] See Terry Eagleton, "It's Time to Abolish the University," unherd.com, August 16, 2023.

faculty and students—a relationship already walking a fine line with respect to boundaries and close relationship and engagement. This de-territorializes and de-ecclesializes the university, destroying the distinction between virtual and real, between word and (inter)action.

These factors, typical of a market-based system, have created new ideological and financial dependencies for universities within a business model that relies on large consultancy firms to develop strategic plans that influence the agenda for teaching as well as research.

All this changing landscape is lost in the eyes of those who see theology only from the perspective of intra-ecclesial fights. The polycrisis of the church can be explained by the demands of part of the laity who call into question the authority of the hierarchy and the pope and, through it, the ecclesiology inherited from the Gregorian revolution (eleventh and twelfth centuries) and Tridentine reform and Counter-Reformation (after the mid-sixteenth century). The problem is that after Vatican II, theology has spent considerable energy in the theologization of *society*, and there is very minimal or sometimes no theology of *institutions*—including ecclesial and ecclesiastical institutions. It has become undesirable, or in any case very hard, for theology to help the church regain some minimal legitimacy as a body both instituted and instituting. The concept of institution applied to the church cannot stop at a philosophical, sociological, or legal concept, but must draw from the theological dimension specific to the church and its historical roots as a sign of the mystery of salvation.

Theology has therefore put itself under threat within another species in danger, that of universities as institutions.[10] Cultural production in contact with the lived religion now operates more

---

[10] See "Global Colloquium of the UNESCO Forum for Higher Education Research and Knowledge" (2006).

and more in society, and less and less within the academy. In the academy, theology has been operationalized within a commercialization of the university, increasingly seen as immediately usable professional training (skills) for the demands of the job market.[11] The reduction of the tradition and transmission of knowledge to transaction, facilitated by technical progress in education technology, has convinced us that we can *know* without spending time learning and living the tradition.[12] The fact is that "required courses in philosophy and theology and the sciences and in literature are not there to sustain departments or because there are endowed chairs. They are required because one can't really be educated if you have never read a book published before, say, 1850."[13]

This risk is even greater for theological scholarship, with its ecclesial concerns and ethos. The general crisis of credibility and authority of our institutions endangers the engagement at the intersection between the past and present of institutions (church, university, theology) in the context of the new "dataist" and transhumanist demagogies crossing democracies, even in the West.[14] Deconstruction is no guarantee of liberation, especially in this phase of this cultural revolution, "this engulfing of culture by the market," "the unplanned and mostly unnoticed obsolescence of this very basic element of the human form of life [when] the

---

[11] See, for example, Tomas Chamorro-Premuzic and Becky Frankiewicz, "6 Reasons Why Higher Education Needs to Be Disrupted," *Harvard Business Review,* November 19, 2019.

[12] On the effects of "presentism" on education, see François Hartog, *Chronos: L'Occident aux prises avec le Temps* (Paris: Gallimard, 2020), esp. chap. 6.

[13] Michael Sean Winters, "Three University Presidents' Failure Is an Opportunity for Catholic Higher Ed," *National Catholic Reporter,* December 13, 2023, on the congressional testimony by the presidents of University of Pennsylvania, Harvard University, and Massachusetts Institute of Technology about anti-Semitism on campus during the Israel-Hamas war that started on October 7, 2023.

[14] See Yuval Harari, *Homo Deus: A Brief History of Tomorrow* (New York: Harper Perennial, 2018).

work of cultural transmission is increasingly being conducted in such a way as to maximize the earnings of those who oversee it."[15] Institutions can give more freedom than spontaneous social and cultural movements.

Roberto Calasso called this time of the dominance of big data a "post-historical era," in which dataism functions as a new form of Gnosticism: "a sort of incessant bricolage of knowledge, without having any certainty about a starting point and without even imagining a starting point of arrival."[16] This new dataist demagogy represents a challenge to contemporary democracy as an attempt to serve humankind according to an ideal of humanity that today is instead treated as available and expendable for the flow of data and algorithms, not to mention AI.[17]

But the expansion of frontier technologies in information also represents a challenge for religious knowledge and theology.[18] Will this "augmented human species" be capable of maintaining its humanity? There is a profound need of a common and shared human vision for growth and interaction. At this juncture academic institutions have a "reserve function" against the naivete of dataist and transhumanist demagogies as well as against the excesses of a twenty-first-century political correctness that attacks Western historical particularity in the name of a claim to universality understood in only a monopolistic way. In the

---

[15] Talbot Brewer, "The Great Malformation: A Personal Skirmish in the Battle for Attention," *The Hedgehog Review* (Summer 2023).

[16] Roberto Calasso, *The Unnamable Present*, trans. Richard Dixon (New York: Farrar Straus, and Giroux, 2019), 32. Originally published in Italian, *L'innominabile attuale* (Milan: Adelphi. 2017).

[17] See Remo Bodei, *Dominio e sottomissione: Schiavi, animali, macchine, Intelligenza Artificiale* (Bologna: Il Mulino, 2019), 319–42.

[18] The World Economic Forum's "Global Risks Report 2023" lists among the most severe risks at the global level for the next decade: misinformation and disinformation; adverse outcomes of frontier technologies (including AI); erosion of social cohesion and societal polarization; digital inequality and lack of access to digital services.

context of identity politics, the criticism against the institutions of the Western world reveals the false universalism of the indictment of the Western world as a whole.[19]

This era of global resentment has only partially spared the Catholic Church and Catholic higher education. It is a resentment against the ecclesiastical system, stemming from the fallout of the sexual-abuse crisis (raising concerns about misuse of authority and power), the refusal to address racism, and the apparent detachment from reality affecting many members of the hierarchy. But there is also an "ecclesioclastic," church-destroying narrative, which also produces a resentment against the ecclesial vocation of Catholic educational institutions: one of the effects of a view of the church that is identified not only historically but essentially with a theology that supported and justified racism, colonialism, and sexism. This resentment creates a new ideology, where every tradition is only oppressive rather than containing some capacity for also liberating elements.

Here a specific new battle front has opened up for theology: the new largely invisible centers of political and intellectual power, more and more in charge of creating, delivering, or denying knowledge through the algorithm, now not only challenge political myths and rituals of our secular modernity, but also the symbolic and religious rituals that cohere the human community at a deeper level, including the ecclesial.[20] From a conception of political power and sovereignty that emerged in

---

[19] See Slavoj Zizek, "Troubles with Identity," *The Philosophical Salon*, May 28, 2018. A quick look at the differences in the historical experience of Christianity between North America and Europe, within North America, and within Europe is enough bring into question the existence of one so-called Western world. Besides the opportunistic transatlantic alliances of a given political moment or election cycle, European populists and nationalists (and Fascists before them) tend to cast a pretty harsh judgement on the effects of Americanization of the old continent in the last hundred years.

[20] See Byung-Chul Han, *The Disappearance of Rituals: A Topology of the Present*, trans. Daniel Steuer (Medford, MA: Polity, 2020).

the clash between church and state between the Middle Ages and the early modern period, we have arrived now at a political imagination that is religious but does not require church and state anymore. Like the institutional church, academic theology too, must awaken from the dream of self-sovereignty.

Theology within Market and *Ecclesia*

The feeling that there was a crisis of the idea of university within Catholic institutions of higher education already had been circulating for some time, visible from the attempts to reshape the mission along the lines of John Henry Newman's *The Idea of a University* (1852).[21] It is one of the effects of the astronomical cost of study in universities, whose survival also depends on students' tolerance for high debt.

It's not just a matter of financial sustainability for students and their families. There is also a sense of unease among those who work in universities, where the technocratic paradigm has led to the domination of influencers and self-taught experts whose authority arises from their roles as columnists and anchors; donors and alumni; political lobbies and their relationship to transnational and sovereign big money rather than the authority of study and the building of knowledge by professors when it comes to determining the soul of the academic community.

Especially in a market-based university system, the authority and voice of theology are inseparable from the economic system in which they operate, and it is a system characterized by the dominance of the economic order over intellectual work.[22] Now, despite the fact that the perspective of faith on the main Catholic campuses tends to be articulated, thanks to Vatican II, in

---

[21] See John Henry Newman, *The Idea of a University*, ed. Ian T. Ker (Oxford: Oxford University Press, 1976).

[22] See the analysis of our post-Weberian world of knowledge by Italian philosopher Massimo Cacciari, *Il lavoro dello spirito* (Milan: Adelphi, 2020).

ecumenical, interreligious, inclusive, and non-proselytizing terms, the status of theology is experiencing a situation of great precariousness—not in the diplomatic language of mission statements, but in the facts of changing power structures. The challenges to the freedom of theological thinking are no longer mainly derived from ecclesiastical control or political control. They now derive from the dislocation of power: from the axis between church and state to the unencumbered power of the market; from the political to the economic; from the bourgeois capitalist model to that of globalization.[23]

What is relevant to the future and the freedom of theology is the institutional church's inertia as well as its capacity for resistance in the face of systemic changes; that is, the institutional church can ignore market forces in a way that academia cannot. This has momentous consequences for the freedom of theological thought. University administrators' solutions to higher-education market trends put Catholic identity at risk, particularly in colleges and universities seeking to emulate the Ivy League schools.

And the neo-traditionalist side of the "culture wars" addresses the question of Catholic identity in an intellectually problematic and deficient way, relying especially on party-political rhetoric and tactics and the uncritical acceptance of new forms of fundamentalism. Overcoming confessionalism in an ecumenical vision of theological studies has been beneficial, but also less transformative than the absorption happening through market mechanisms.

The Catholic ecclesial and ecclesiastical ecosystem is, whether we like it or not, the water in which both Catholic schools (including colleges and universities) and the intellectual and theological world still swim, and it is an ecclesial system

---

[23] For important international perspectives, see *Theology and the University*, ed. Fáinche Ryan, Dirk Ansorge, Josef Quitterer (New York: Routledge, 2024).

characterized by a strong clerical imprint. But this leads to a failure to recognize new systems of control over the freedom of Catholic theology. As Catholic university theologians and professors of other departments fear the return of control and surveillance by the ecclesiastical hierarchies on the freedom of research, technocrats have already occupied universities with a more subtle kind of tyranny. There is an anti-humanities ideology driving university governance that no amount of enrollment, or majors and minors, will abate.

Mission statements of universities and of departments of humanities and liberal arts, but also of theology and religious studies, have often become the fig leaf covering a political order or an economic system effectively replacing the human and divine sciences with the "hard sciences"—especially as business and law schools shift into the center of gravity of the university—not only financial and politically, but morally and symbolically. The institutions of research and scholarship, their form and language, no longer depend on the ecclesiastical or the political, but on the market, on the economic. At the same time there remain a small number of universities "wealthy enough to prioritize all manner of values that are plausibly averse to their bottom line."[24]

This political order and economic system has not only marginalized theology and the disciplines without which theology cannot survive (philosophy, classics, foreign languages, history, literature, arts), but has also changed the very idea of an academic profession—even for those starting out or who are in the middle of a career as a theologian—from the ideal of absolute dedication to research and teaching work to the precariousness of adjunct or permanent positions without the protection of tenure. These have serious consequences, not only on the profession but also on freedom of research, creating an existential

---

[24] Greg Conti, "The Rise of the Sectarian University," *Compact Magazine*, December 28, 2023.

situation for many who teach, but also who personally represent and embody theology today. The "adjunctification" of faculty in theology and religious studies (as in other disciplines) means a very heavy teaching load, no office space, little or no interaction with colleagues, stern intimations from university administrators threatening jobs and contract renewals while overfocusing on evaluations and industrial output of teaching and grading and limiting support for research and academic writing. There is a fundamental incompatibility between the adjunctification of the university and the Catholic intellectual tradition, but also between adjunctification and the role Catholic higher education aspires to play in our national conversation on social and economic justice.[25]

This is part of the broader process of contractualization of work, which includes the theologian in its wake. The contract is no longer related to the calling and profession entailed in a commitment to and with the church or the civil community. Other counterparts of the market in the name of "lucrative conformism" affect the intellectual and academic establishment in an ascendant academic capitalist knowledge/learning regime expressed in faculty work, departmental activity, and administrative behavior.[26]

This involves a radical redefinition of the idea of religious, spiritual, and emotional formation and education, which now has been reduced to ongoing professional training. Not only academics are affected by a market approach to education and training, but also religious personnel in ministerial roles—ordained clergy, instituted ministry, or "simply" lay roles—in the church.

---

[25] See John-Paul Heil and Stephen McGinley, "Core Fellows: Addressing the Catholic Intellectual Tradition's Incompatibility with Adjunctification," *Journal of Catholic Higher Education* 40, no. 2 (2021): 163–74.

[26] See Sheila Slaughter and Gary Rhoades, *Academic Capitalism and the New Economy: Markets, State, and Higher Education* (Baltimore: Johns Hopkins University Press, 2004).

This crisis of diminishment of intellectual work and of theology as a vocation (both professional and ecclesial) comes with the growth of a demagogic component favoring digital communication collapsing the credibility of institutional religion—already troubled following the sex-abuse crisis—and by manipulation by theological-political agendas with little or no *sensus ecclesiae*.

The crisis of academic theology, aggravated by the political and ecclesial situation, has transitioned from "ecclesiocentrism" (still dominant until Vatican II, and even today in some areas) to the seductions of "ecclesioclasm" of particular schismatic options, particularly sectarianism and neo-Gnosticism.

Ecclesiology is at risk of becoming a desperate "ecclesiodicy": the pressure, in light of the daily news of financial and sexual scandals, to justify or find for the church the reasons for existing as a historical organization established by Christ. This also affects academic theology. In the long run the situation of mutual estrangement and alienation between the institutional Catholic Church and theology will endanger theology more than the institutional church ever could. The institutional church has resources (financial, political, symbolic) to survive this upheaval that academic theology simply does not.

On one hand, the current upheaval means that the relationships between academic theology and ecclesial institutions are no longer the same as in the first post–Vatican II period (Paul VI), or even the same as in the second post-conciliar period (John Paul II and Benedict XVI). Francis's pontificate led to a much-welcomed truce in the tensions between theology and the magisterium, though it didn't lessen the gap between the two.

On the other hand, "marketization" has fostered a crisis of authority within academic theology, from different and coexisting pressures: commodification and the technocratic paradigm in higher education; the collapse of institutional curricular support, student interest, and publication subsidies in the humanities; the erosion of Catholicism at a popular level; and lately, the combined rejection of the theological establishment by populism and neo-traditionalism that are part of today's diversity.

These forces are not going away anytime soon—and when they go, they will have done considerable damage to the role of theology and religious-studies departments, as well as damaging the moral and intellectual standing of the discipline. The ghosting of theology in Catholic higher education does not affect seminaries to the same extent.[27] And this could bring a growing clericalization of theology that flows in the veins of an institutional church increasingly driven by concerns and visions of the world that are profoundly different from the concerns of Catholic universities. Catholic seminaries also hold economic and systemic advantage in competition with academic theologians in non-seminary Catholic higher education.

This is the result of the total insertion of humanistic and religious knowledge into the economic and productivity system that at the same time alienates theology from the scientific disciplines, where the latter follow, even in Catholic universities, a trajectory created by public universities and the Ivy League. As Alasdair MacIntyre writes:

> The most prestigious Catholic universities often mimic the structures and goals of the most prestigious secular universities and do so with little sense of something having gone seriously amiss to the extent that this is so the institutional prospects for the future history of the Catholic philosophical tradition are not encouraging.[28]

This absorption of theology and Catholic universities into the technocratic paradigm is accompanied by a near-total

---

[27] See Katarina Schuth, *Seminary Formation: Recent History–Current Circumstances–New Directions* (Collegeville, MN: Liturgical Press, 2016).

[28] Alasdair C. MacIntyre, *God, Philosophy, Universities: A Selective History of the Catholic Philosophical Tradition* (Lanham, MD: Rowman & Littlefield, 2009), 179.

estrangement between the hierarchical leadership of the church and the theological and cultural debate. This phenomenon continues a certain anti-intellectual tradition within the American clerical system, already denounced as problematic as early as the 1950s by John Tracy Ellis.[29] But in the current historical moment for the church, this estrangement has amplified effects as bishops and their seminaries are distanced from the broad intellectual and scientific debate—even in the most basic ways, such as we've seen in some polemics during the COVID-19 pandemic, where vocal Catholic influencers argued against masking and then also against vaccines.

The Traditionalist Responses
to Technocracy

The mutual alienation of theology and church presents a serious problem for both sides. The work of Catholic theologians is increasingly viewed as less relevant (or worse, completely irrelevant) to many church leaders—not just bishops, but also donors and others with various kinds of influence. Some have turned attention and charitable giving instead to initiatives that further the ideology of the "culture wars."

These new initiatives are startups within the theological economy that express a rejection of mainstream academic theological knowledge. Add to that a certain Catholic following coalescing around some of the big players in politics and culture. It is as though the three "publics" that David Tracy saw theology addressing[30] have now been reduced to two: the academy and the church, which has been subsumed into the partisan divides of American social and political life.

---

[29] See John Tracy Ellis, "American Catholics and Intellectual Life," *Thought* 30 (Autumn 1955): 351–88.

[30] See Tracy, *The Analogical Imagination*, 5.

The anti-Vatican II or non-Vatican II versions of the otherwise important call to the rediscovery of the beauty of the Catholic tradition comes at a long-term cost for the church. The result of the "culture wars" in the church and theology is not only a theologization of different political ideologies, but a "culturalization," in a politically partisan sense, of every theological question. The theological debate has focused on a current cultural canon of social issues and has largely stopped drawing from the sources of the theological tradition in its entirety— catholicity chronologically (the whole time span of the tradition) and geographically (not just Europe and the West) understood.

On the left, there was first a transition from theology to religious studies, and then from religious studies to cultural anthropology and ethnography; this shift discouraged many young Catholics from exploring conciliar and post-conciliar theology, or rather it encouraged them to reject this change in method and ethos and to embrace neo-traditionalism. On the conservative side of the spectrum, off-campus anti-university and anti-theological initiatives have come from fundamentalist and neo-traditionalist Catholic circles supported by bishops and strong private donors. This is accompanied, within Catholic universities, by the phenomenon of a de-theologization of the knowledge of militant Catholicism—part of the larger phenomenon of questioning academia today, as mass culture destroys both popular culture and high culture.[31]

Liberal and progressive theology pays a price for refusing to take seriously the institutional question in the ecclesiology of Vatican II in the post-conciliar period; post-conciliar ecclesiological pluralism has predominantly excluded visions of church that did not abandon themselves to new extra-ecclesiastical and idealized visions of society, a new version of the ideology of the

---

[31] See Christopher Lasch, *Culture de masse ou culture populaire?* (Castelnau-le-Lez, Hérault: Climats, 2001).

societas perfecta. At the same time, Catholic historiography has embraced the turn toward the social, cultural, and anthropological, which is not a problem in itself but becomes one when it displays a growing resentment and rejection of any institutional dimension of the church.[32]

The simple fact is that students interested in taking theology courses in Catholic universities are those who really want to "be Catholic," seeking something more openly and ecclesially Catholic from theology departments and programs. They are interested in the sense of wonderment, in a voyage of exploration that the intellectual and theological tradition as a living, ecclesial *corpus* can arouse. And they are less interested in postmodernist, deconstructionist dead ends, which, as essential as they are to understanding the tradition, easily become another sort of antiquarianism.

But now this demand for the living tradition is being answered with a supply of voices and products coming mainly from institutions with anti-Vatican II, neo-conservative, or neo-traditionalist theological views. This is part of the global *revanche de Dieu* (revenge of God) and will not disappear anytime soon. This theological revanchism does not just come from a few fringe intellectuals, but is part of a larger phenomenon, a new search for Catholic identity that takes various forms. It can sometimes be expressed as enthusiasm for the Tridentine mass and disgust with the Novus Ordo. Or it can take the form of an interest in countercultural communities, such a some version of the Benedict Option. But it can also take the form of a theo-political imagination that rejects liberal democracy in favor

---

[32] See the methodological turn impressed upon Catholic historiography in the United States by, among others, Robert Orsi, *The Madonna of 115th Street: Faith and Community in Italian Harlem, 1880–1950* (New Haven, CT: Yale University Press, 1985); see also the sharp observations by Enzo Traverso, *Singular Pasts: The "I" in Historiography*, trans. Adam Schoene (New York: Columbia University Press, 2022), esp. 139–43.

of a new Christianity that draws inspiration from an imagined theology and culture of the Middle Ages. This idealizing is often mixed with ethnocentric and nationalist suspicion toward those Catholics or Christians who come from parts of the world where Christianity is not the predominant religion.

The rise of this renewed anti-modernism marks a regression in the ability of Catholics to understand the problem of the state and politics in our age.[33] But it also says something about the state of Catholic theology. And we cannot assume that the institutions that support academic theology will last forever. For Catholic theology to be healthy, it cannot depend entirely on a few large, wealthy universities. Nor can it even express itself in the ecclesial sphere only through seminars for the training of diocesan clergy or religious orders—whether in theology or church management. It requires the smaller Catholic colleges to remain a vital part of our ecclesial and civil communities.

This must be seen in the context of the struggle for the future of Catholicism, where regaining the command levers of the institutional church is seen as an objective of what I call, for lack of a better term, the anti-Vatican II agenda. The neo-traditionalist revenge in the Catholic Church sees not only Pope Francis, but also Vatican II and the advancements of Catholic theology since Vatican II, as something to be rejected, revoked.[34]

Academic Theology in Global Catholicism

Since Vatican II the position of theology has changed significantly both within the ecclesial educational and intellectual system

---

[33] See Patrick J. Deneen, *Why Liberalism Failed* (New Haven, CT: Yale University Press, 2019).

[34] See Catherine Clifford and Massimo Faggioli, "Introduction," in *The Oxford Handbook of Vatican II*, ed. Catherine Clifford and Massimo Faggioli (Oxford: Oxford University Press, 2023), 1–6.

and in the secularized system of the university and intellectual
world: its role in society, in the academy, and in the church. The
most significant changes consisted not only in the de-clerical-
ization of knowledge in the church, but also in the emergence
of a post-ecclesial horizon and the imposition and acceptance
of the "technocratic paradigm" within educational and training
institutions. As Pope Francis puts it in *Laudato Si'*: "It can be said
that many problems of today's world stem from the tendency,
at times unconscious, to make the method and aims of science
and technology an epistemological paradigm which shapes the
lives of individuals and the workings of society" (no. 107). In the
world of knowledge we had the emergence of the technocratic
paradigm and its tools—in ways that are new compared to the
birth of the modern university in the nineteenth century, "the
mandarins of the lab" in the universities of European imperial
powers.[35] To this has corresponded, in theology, the eclipse of the
horizon of the "history of salvation" in favor of other horizons.[36]

The phenomenon has consequences that go beyond the
confines of Catholic higher education in the United States
or the Anglo-American world and raises questions for global
Catholic theology. The institutional crisis of the church, which
goes far beyond the sex-abuse scandal, is no longer just a crisis
of authority, but of legitimacy of the ecclesial dimension, of its
justifiability—not only *ad extra*, but also *ad intra*. The crisis of
receptivity to Vatican II opened the way for a collapse of the
sensus ecclesiae, producing a landscape of different and opposing

---

[35] See Paul Reitter and Chad Wellmon, *Permanent Crisis: The Humanities in
a Disenchanted Age* (Chicago: University of Chicago Press; 2021), 113–51.

[36] See Mariano Delgado, "Mysterium Salutis als innovativer systematischer
Ansatz im Anschluss an das Zweite Vatikanische Konzil," in *La reception du
Concile Vatican II par les theologiens suisses. Die Rezeption des II Vaticanums durch
Schweizer Theologen*, ed. Guy Bedouelle and Mariano Delgado (Fribourg: Aca-
demic Press Fribourg, 2011), 167–78.

"ecclesioclastic"ideologies, in the face of which an apologetic "ecclesiodicy" has become a blunt weapon.[37]

This crisis of legitimacy of the ecclesial dimension has an impact on Catholic theology, which on the one hand is produced, on the public scene, less and less by intellectuals and more and more by a new type of lay person—specialized personnel (lawyers, journalists, politicians, managers) whose claim of a distance from the academy is considered a badge of honor. On the other hand, Catholic universities in the United States and Europe continue to be hubs of the global church to which students and clergy from various parts of the world flock, bringing questions of ecclesiality to Catholic theology that the academic system is not always able or willing to answer.

The neo-conservative and neo-traditionalist side addresses the question of the Catholic identity of theology in ways that have serious problems related to intellectual sustainability, but that aspect of the Catholic theological and cultural spectrum enjoys a kind of "natural monopoly" on certain types of Catholics and by default has a partner in the clerical institution. Those in the neo-conservative camps of Catholic theology lay claim to a series of alternatives, which create false and extreme choices: between the retreat of the Benedict Option and dissolution; between neo-integralism and the extremisms of the politically correct; between clericalist institutionalism and a post-ecclesial horizon.[38]

---

[37] For an example of the crisis of the institutional reception of Vatican II, see the structure and spirit of *The Word on Fire Vatican II Collection*, foreword by Bishop Robert Barron and commentary by the postconciliar popes (Washington, DC: Word on Fire, 2021).

[38] In one of the most interesting passages in his book on the present Catholic moment, Jean-Luc Marion writes: "Today, it is time that we French Catholics take the measure of our responsibilities, past and to come. And that we finally ask forgiveness of the universal Church for, more than others, having inoculated it with its two most recent heresies—integralism and progressivism—each of which, in recent moments, has nearly led to a schism, in France and elsewhere." Jean-Luc Marion, *A Brief Apology for a Catholic Moment* (Chicago: University of Chicago Press, 2021), 13.

But the future of Catholic theology cannot be separated from the future of Catholic universities. And the history of colleges and universities of the Protestant traditions serve as a warning as their universities have been unable to maintain their religious identities in a chronologically rapid passage from the Protestant establishment to a different type of establishment, one absent the dimension of faith.[39]

There is no doubt that the Catholic theological establishment in academia is undergoing a redefinition of its size and role. The choice to ignore these profound global movements could mean a return to theology pre–Vatican II: the prerogative of clerical personnel, with the difference that now there are many fewer ordained clerics and among these even fewer interested in the study of theology. The crisis of the Catholic mission of Catholic universities and their theology departments is not just a crisis of theology, but also a symptom of a broader crisis of "theology of the laity."[40] The detachment of many lay people from the idea of a wider participation in the mission of the institutional church is part of the ongoing eclipse of political utopias and part of the crisis of our democracies.[41]

Catholic theology or theology in Catholic academic institutions needs an expanded vision, once more centered on the Easter event and rooted in exegesis, patrology, history, and hermeneutics. It needs a theology capable of practical, active reflection and expression, compelling personal practices, and engagement in social and political life in ways that engage with but don't entrust the study of theology to other fields—psychology,

---

[39] See George M. Marsden, *The Soul of the American University: From Protestant Establishment to Established Nonbelief* (New York: Oxford University Press, 1994).

[40] See Grant Kaplan, "The Crisis in Catholic Theology," *America*, May 19, 2021; see also Marco Vergottini, *Il cristiano testimone: Congedo dalla teologia del laicato* (Bologna: EDB, 2017).

[41] See Enzo Traverso, *Revolution: An Intellectual History* (London: Verso, 2021).

sociology, ethnology, anthropology. And Catholic theology needs a stabilizing, unifying, and prospective vision that has been lacking during the downsizing of Christian churches. The field of theological study is at a crossroads.

The detachment of academic theology from the control of the institutional church was one of the most important achievements in the post–Vatican II church because it gave freedom to intellectual inquiry. It is not realistic to imagine that Catholic academic theology will return as catechesis or the voice of the institutional church, or even return to the old apologetics. But academic theology in global Catholicism will have to become more ecclesial in the sense of being more aware of the expectations of today's Catholics, especially the younger generations.

There can be no detachment from the institutional church that does not also involve a certain detachment from the true people of God. The fate of Catholic religious knowledge is inseparable, at least in the Western world, from the fate of academic theology. To survive and thrive, theology needs universities and (lay) students, professional associations and societies, publishers, and journals. One can imagine that the church could survive intellectually without academic theology, but it would certainly be not only the poorer for it, but also the more miserable, incapable of reading, interpreting, and interacting with the signs of the times.

Compared to the recent past, the system in which knowledge operates today means more market and less state. In the case of religious and theological knowledge, it even means less church. This is a step farther than theology's legitimate claims to academic freedom. Once theology became less "churchlike," especially in the United States, it became even less critical because of the supporting role it played in a system of cultural production.[42]

---

[42] See Terry Eagleton, *The Idea of Culture* (Oxford: Blackwell, 2009); id., *Culture and the Death of God* (New Haven, CT: Yale University Press, 2015).

Among its tasks, theology serves the church, but in practice in many parts of the Western world it has largely ceased this work with the church as part of the *sentire cum ecclesia*—thinking with the church. Today, both the magisterium and the people of God are looking like very distant speaking partners for theology. This change does not bring greater authority to theological scholarship. In finding greater freedom from ecclesiastical control, theology has met with new and less visible subjections and subjugations that are changing its course.

6

Proposals for a Way Forward

Without committing to one particular and idiosyncratic theological worldview, I have always tried in my life and work as a scholar to hold in creative tension, distinct but not separated, church and world, theology and history, academic and public scholarship. I came into the university as a citizen of the world but also as an active member of the church. In the year 1989, I was a freshman at the secular University of Bologna. And my American experience, following my move to the United States in 2008, has been a blessing, generously expanding my framework of references—historical, theological, but also ecclesial.

This effort at synthesis, keeping distinct arenas that nevertheless are not separated, has since the beginning of the millennium become more complicated. The disruption of the international order has accelerated, and the role of religions has more and more been perceived as part of the problem rather than the solution; arguing in favor of theology in the university is seen by some as ivory-tower elitism or petty and self-serving.

But religious traditions, churches, and the Catholic Church in particular, play a key role on the world map where the secular and the post-secular alternate without a precise order, as random images and videos do on digital platforms. And a church without theology, "faith seeking understanding," is not imaginable. Nor is a theology without some kind of robust professional, academic research role imaginable. And there is no theology without some kind of vital connection of theology *with* the church. Academic theology in universities with an ecclesial connection also hold social, moral, ethical responsibility—among the most effective arguments for the development of the role of religion for a peaceful coexistence in our multireligious and multicultural societies.

Even so, as we've seen, theology faces a very uncertain future. Not only are public officials questioning state support for the humanities in public universities, but there is also a kind of impatience growing in Catholic universities, often aided by outside consultants and consulting firms, which is putting cherished departments of liberal arts on the chopping block. An entire world of knowledge is facing headwinds, and students are fleeing to majors more closely aligned to employment.

Academic theology faces a similar situation, with some key differences and ecclesial and ecclesiological consequences. In his last lecture Richard Gaillardetz pointed to three major factors in pursuing "meaningful and lasting ecclesial reform": re-engaging with the institutional dimension of the church; finding a "reflective equilibrium" between trust and suspicion of the tradition; realizing the "sense of the faithful." A few months later the secretary general of the Vatican's International Theological Commission, Fr. Piero Coda, stated that "there is no reform of the church without reform of theology."[1] An important test for the ability of theology to contribute to church reform is the Synod on Synodality and its reception in the global church.[2]

---

[1] Piero Coda, "Non c'è riforma della Chiesa senza riforma della teologia" [there is no reform of the church without reform of theology], *L'Osservatore Romano*, July 23, 2023.

[2] See Richard R. Gaillardetz, "Loving and Reforming a Holy Yet Broken Church," lecture, Boston College, September 23, 2022.

My proposal for a revisioning of the role of theology *in* and *for* Catholic higher education focuses on three factors: the relationship between academic theology and the church; a new coherent vision around Vatican II; a new engagement with the tradition.

First, a *re-engagement of university theology with the institutional dimension and life of the church* is critical. The current wave of anti-institutionalism of Catholics isn't the same as that of the 1970s; today, it is part and parcel of the Catholic disruption seen in the daily news feed about the sexual-abuse crisis, the financial scandals, and the cultural and pastoral lack of awareness by many in church leadership—and carries similarities to the current sentiment toward universities' administrators. But both anti-Vatican II and non-Vatican II Catholicism have a narrative and a strategy based on understanding the necessity of institutions (in the church and in the university). Addressing these is a challenge that theologians need to take seriously and respond to. The price for ignoring the disruptive strategies may well mean theology itself (not just Vatican II) will return to a landscape similar to previous decades, with the preservation of a self-interested and self-absorbed clerical clique—only now with few ordained clerics in its ranks. More generally, this could also mean leaving Vatican II to the mercy of an institutional church and a seminary system withdrawing and more alienated from theology. This is a price Catholic scholars (theologians and historians) pay in their temptation to avoid anything that sounds "institutional," choosing instead to swim with the tide of an anti-institutionalism that seeks to be relevant and gravitates toward "cultural studies."

It is essential that academic theologians find new ways to cultivate and engage the ecclesial nature of theological work. Higher education's current pattern of detachment and disengagement is not sustainable. Re-engagement does not mean Catholic academic theology becomes the "think tank" of the bishops, the voice of the institutional church, or goes back to old-style apologetics. But the failure of Catholic theologians to cultivate the specifically *ecclesial* context, nature, and mission of theology is self-defeating, leaving Catholic theology increasingly vulnerable not just to cultural trendiness, but also to becoming overrun by the technocratic paradigm and displaced by neo-traditionalist, neo-conservative versions of Catholic identity. At the same time, Catholic theology must reflect on the long-term consequences of the assumption that teaching, scholarship, and service in Catholic higher education are a natural progression of political activism for social justice.

Second, we need *a new coherent vision around Vatican II*, because the old ones are gone.[3] There are teachings of Vatican II that clearly require augmentation and development. Some of that work has already been done. Some has not—especially related to women and ministry in the church. Beyond merely two factions of an anti-Vatican II or pre-Vatican II Catholicism, the real problem is a "non-Vatican II, non-conciliar Catholicism" that denies the *living* tradition. "Non-Vatican II" proponents do not simply ignore Vatican II, but they seek above all to neutralize it, considering the trajectories of Vatican II concluded and exhausted, its promises empty. This critical rethinking of both the hypostatization and the dismissal of Vatican II begins in scholarly conversations, in classrooms, and in critical decisions regarding the future of departments and schools of theology.

As academics, we are called to distinguish carefully between different forms of criticism and endorsement of Vatican II. Not all criticism of Vatican II is anti-conciliar, and not all endorsements of Vatican II are conciliar. Vatican II theology must go beyond the "monumentalization" of the council, which

---

[3] See Catherine Clifford and Massimo Faggioli, "Introduction," in *The Oxford Handbook of Vatican II*, ed. Catherine Clifford and Massimo Faggioli, 1–6 (Oxford: Oxford University Press, 2023).

attempts to neutralize the discontinuities, ignores the effects of individualistic post-ecclesial hermeneutics, and attempts to create pages in the book of "civil religion," politicizing memories in the West.

Third, *a new engagement with the tradition* (of which Vatican II is part), also as *paradosis*, not only as critical deconstruction (which is an integral part of the work of academic theology) requires rethinking of both the hypostatization and the dismissal of Vatican II, in order to leave behind the spurious myths and anti-myths of the conciliar teaching and event. We have an opportunity to begin a new phase of fundamental education on the importance of Vatican II *and* the post–Vatican II period within the whole of the Catholic tradition: the both/and instead of the either/or; the old together with the new; the paradoxical and the fragmented; the universal and the particular; the metaphysical and the historical.

Before John Paul II, many considered doctrinal and liturgical questions settled, and both anti-Vatican II traditionalists and post–Vatican II progressives were excluded from the definitive (that is, not infallible) magisterium. The globalization of Catholicism makes clear there is no end of history—not even for doctrinal development.

History has restarted, also within the church, where once-marginalized groups have challenged even the baseline consensus created by John Paul II around Vatican II. Historical consciousness has evaporated; hermeneutical nuances have been lost. A view of cultures that sees them as radically internally hybridized or radically contingent has made dialogue between church and world or faith and culture not just impossible, but pointless. The Catholic theological guild's turn toward political theology, political theory, and identity politics now tends to avoid the fundamental questions: What is the point of believing? Why be a disciple? And this doesn't even take into account other questions around the reduction of ecclesiology to "ecclesiodicy," in light of the identification of the church by default with evil—from patriarchal abuse to cultural genocide. The question today is how to fulfill the most authentic task of theologians, that is, to "give an explanation to anyone who asks you for a reason for your hope" (1 Peter 3:15, my translation).

In the twenty-first century, Catholic theology is "done" more and more in different kinds of institutions—pontifical, Catholic with different orientations, Catholic centers and institutes in non-Catholic institutions, and more—with also many ways to ignore or receive and further develop the vision of theology coming from Pope Francis.[4] But the central question for the future of Catholic theology today remains: How can theology be academically rigorous, critical, scientific, and at the same time committedly ecclesial? These two dimensions are in a tension that can be dynamic and fruitful, even as many institutions today do not see them as coexisting well—or even having the potential to coexist.

Coexistence is possible if we take seriously the unfolding Catholic tradition in all its dynamism, its cultural and historical varieties, in a global vision that is committedly ecumenical and not exclusive of study of other religious and philosophical and intellectual traditions; and if we approach the tradition as something worth trying to understand as well as also worth passing on (*tradere*). This needs careful, informed, and intellectually generous digestion, scrutiny, interrogation, curiosity, appreciation—rather than jumping straight into deconstructive rejection or apologetical application.

It is important to begin by asking whether Catholic universities still aspire to be *universitas* in a way other universities cannot.

---

[4] See Massimo Faggioli, "Theology between the University and the Church as a 'Field Hospital,'" in *Theology and the University*, ed. Fáinche Ryan, Dirk Ansorge, and Josef Quitterer, 39–54 (New York: Routledge, 2024).

In this sense, paradoxically, the irrelevance of theology is exactly its relevance:

> Those who are truly contemporary, who truly belong to their time, are those who neither perfectly coincide with it nor adjust themselves to its demands. They are in this sense irrelevant. But precisely because of this condition, precisely through this disconnection and this anachronism, they are more capable than others of perceiving and grasping their own time.[5]

A church without theology—without faith seeking understanding, in the classic definition—is at risk of becoming a body exposed to the political, social, and economic alliances of the day. A Catholic theology without its roots planted in the real church, without a view to helping the people of God address the spiritual (not only social and political) pressing issues of our time, is at risk of becoming a subsidized, high-cost, self-referential club. The way in which theology speaks of the church is part of its Christian character and an indicator of its moral and spiritual health: "Ultraspiritualism generates materialism, because both live in the bad infinity of the immediate."[6]

Theology is evidently no longer at the heart of the contemporary university. But the need for theology hasn't changed, even if many see theology today as understanding the world by wandering *around* it. But if anything, it is more important than ever.[7]

---

[5] Giorgio Agamben, "What Is the Contemporary?" in *What Is an Apparatus? And Other Essays*, trans. David Kushik and Stefan Pedatella (Stanford, CA: Stanford University Press, 2009), 40.

[6] Italo Mancini, *Tornino i volti* (Genoa: Marietti, 1989), 76 (translation mine).

[7] For some key insights on the challenges of AI, transhumanism, and the virtual world for religion and theology, see Roberto Calasso, *The Unnamable Present*, trans. Richard Dixon (New York: Farrar Straus and Giroux, 2019), chap. 1; original in Italian, *L'innominabile attuale* (Milan: Adelphi 2017).

One of the ways to reposition it in a less marginal role, especially in Catholic higher education, is to claim a commitment to theology as faith working with reason in an incarnational-sacramental imagination—a new phase in the *aggiornamento* of Vatican II, with an ethos that continues to be critical but dares to be unapologetically ecclesial.

Acknowledgments

The goal of this book has not been to offer a systematic treatise on the role or the future of Catholic theology in the university, but rather to contribute, from a historical and ecclesiological perspective, to the reflections of all those—especially for academic theologians, faculty members, or administrators who now feel they are being brought to reckoning at this moment in the history of higher education. This book is the fruit of considerations coming from my experience as a professor in Catholic universities in the United States, my previous study and work in Europe, as well as my exchanges with colleagues and students from many different countries.

The work leading to this book was supported by the College of Liberal Arts and Sciences at Villanova University with the research semester granted to me in the fall semester of 2023. During that semester I had the opportunity to exchange ideas with colleagues at the Université Catholique de Louvain (Louvain-la-Neuve, Belgium), where I resided in October and November 2023 as holder of the Francqui Chair; in those weeks I had important conversations and found important points of convergence within the debates on the role of theology in two different continents, the role of Catholic universities, and the differences in Catholic histories on these continents. I want to thank here in particular my colleagues at UCL: Geert Van Oyen, Jean-Marie Auwers, Mehdi Azaiez, Catherine Chevalier, Jean-Pascal Gay, Arnaud Join-Lambert, Walter Lesch, and Olivier Riaudel. My dear friend Louis de Strycker has been a very important point of reference and support for many years, even before our first in-person meeting in Brussels.

In the last few years I had in-depth exchanges with colleagues at the Loyola Institute at Trinity College Dublin, where we started a conversation at the 2016 conference, "The Role of the Church in Pluralist Society," and then continued at the 2022 conference, "Theology and the University." I am especially thankful to Cornelius Casey, Fáinche Ryan, and Michael Joseph Kirwan for their hospitality and openness to addressing difficult topics in complicated times.

I benefited from the conversations with my Italian colleagues of the Associazione Teologica Italiana, at the congress in Naples of September 2021, "Fare teologia per questo mondo, per questo tempo" (Doing theology for this world, for this time). In Italy, Antonio Ballarò and Serena Noceti have been precious conversation partners and friends over a long period of time.

Before those conversations in Europe, these questions and conversations started with my colleagues in the United States in my roles as a co-founder and then steering committee member (2012–23) of the Vatican II Studies unit at the American Academy of Religion; as a panelist for the session "Catholic Theology and the Contemporary University" at the annual convention of the Catholic Theological Society of America in Pittsburgh (June 2019); as a speaker at the conference "Vatican II and Catholic Higher Education: Leading Forward" at Sacred Heart University (October 2022) and also at "Lighting the Way Forward: The Purpose of Catholic Higher Education in a Changing World" at the University of San Diego (January 2024).

In the last few years the European Academy of Religion, with its annual conferences, beginning in 2017 in Bologna, has become an important encounter between different theological and academic cultures within the global community of colleges and universities. The frequent meetings and workshops organized by the network for an intercontinental, multi-volume commentary of Vatican II, started by Peter Hünermann, have given me essential perspectives about challenges Catholic theology is facing globally.

These pages are the fruit of fifteen years of personal exchanges and dialogue with a larger network of colleagues—teaching, writing, coordinating, co-editing, and organizing, especially in North America and Australia. These colleagues include Gerald Beyer; Timothy Brunk; Thomas Cattoi; Catherine Clifford; Kevin DePrinzio, OSA; Bryan Froehle; David Gibson; Mark Graham; Timothy Hanchin; Christiane Lang Hearlson; Michael Hollerich; Kevin Hughes; Jennifer Jackson; Richard Lennan; Rafael Luciani; John Martens; Mark Massa, SJ; James McEvoy; Michael Murphy; David O'Brien; Ormond Rush; Carlos Schickendantz; Gerald Schlabach; Stephen Schloesser, SJ; Ethan Schwartz; Rachel Smith; Michael Sean Winters; Stephanie Wong; and Jonathan Yates.

Tony Godzieba, Edward Hahnenberg, and Jaisy Joseph deserve special thanks for reading portions of this book. I am very grateful for their suggestions and generous willingness to be part of a communal process of discerning scholarship. My editor at Orbis Books, Lil Copan, has followed this project very closely, in all its stages, with great care. All opinions, omissions, and errors remain my own, *ça va sans dire*.

Last, but not least, I wish to express my gratitude to all my colleagues in the Department of Theology and Religious Studies and the students at Villanova University, where lively conversations on these topics have enormously enriched my experience as a teacher, writer, and citizen of the university.

Bibliography

Agamben, Giorgio. *The Kingdom and the Glory: For a Theological Genealogy of Economy and Government*. Stanford, CA: Stanford University Press, 2012. Original Italian:Vicenza: Neri Pozza, 2007.

————. "What Is the Contemporary?" In *What Is an Apparatus? And Other Essays*, translated by David Kushik and Stefan Pedatella, 39–56. Stanford, CA: Stanford University Press, 2009. Original Italian: *Che cos'è il contemporaneo?* Rome: Nottetempo, 2008.

Ahern, Kevin. "Charism, Crisis and Adaptation: A Theological Reading of Identity in Catholic Higher Education." *Journal of Catholic Higher Education* 40, no. 2 (2021): 111–27.

Alberigo, Giuseppe, Jean-Pierre Jossua, and Joseph A. Komonchak, eds. *The Reception of Vatican II*. Washington, DC: Catholic University of America Press, 1987.

Alberigo Giuseppe, and Joseph A. Komonchak. *History of Vatican II*, 5 vols. Maryknoll, NY: Orbis Books, 1995–2006. Published also in Italian, French, German, Spanish, Portuguese, and Russian.

Anderson, Benedict R.O'G. *Imagined Communities: Reflections on the Origin and Spread of Nationalism*. London:Verso, 2006; first edition 1983.

Andraos, Michel, and Anthony John Baptist, Geraldo L. De Mori, Stefanie Knauss, eds. "Theology and Higher Education" *Concilium* 5 (2023).

Arendt, Hannah. *Men in Dark Times.* New York: Harcourt, Brace & World, 1968.

———. *The Human Condition.* Chicago: University of Chicago Press, 1958.

Barone, Christian, and Michael Czerny. *Siblings All, Sign of the Times: The Social Teaching of Pope Francis.* Maryknoll, NY: Orbis Books, 2022.

Beard, Mary. *Confronting the Classics: Traditions, Adventures and Innovations.* New York: Norton, 2013.

Berlant, Lauren. *Cruel Optimism.* Durham, NC: Duke University Press, 2011.

Beyer, Gerald J. *Just Universities: Catholic Social Teaching Confronts Corporatized Higher Education.* New York: Fordham University Press, 2021.

Bodei, Remo. *Dominio e sottomissione: Schiavi, animali, macchine, intelligenza artificiale.* Bologna: Il Mulino, 2019.

Bonta Moreland, Anna, and Mark Shiffman. "Educating for What? Liberal Arts in a Professional World." In *Catholic Higher Education and Catholic Social Thought*, edited by Bernard G. Prusak and Jennifer Reed-Bouley, 99–125. Mahwah, NJ: Paulist Press, 2023.

Borghesi, Massimo. *Catholic Discordance: Neoconservatism vs. the Field Hospital Church of Pope Francis*, translated by Barry Hudock. Collegeville, MN: Liturgical Press, 2021.

———. *The Mind of Pope Francis: Jorge Mario Bergoglio's Intellectual Journey*, translated by Barry Hudock. Collegeville, MN: Liturgical Press, 2018.

Brewer, Talbot. "The Great Malformation: A Personal Skirmish in the Battle for Attention." *The Hedgehog Review* (Summer 2023).

Briel, Don J., Kenneth E. Goodpaster, Michael Naughton. *What We Hold in Trust: Rediscovering the Purpose of Catholic Higher Education.* Washington, DC: Catholic University of America Press, 2021.

Bua, Pasquale, "La Gregoriana e il Concilio. Il contributo dei teologi dell'Università al Vaticano II." *Gregorianum* 96, no. 2, (2015): 319–43.

Burton, Tara Isabella. "Rational Magic: Why a Silicon Valley Culture That Was Once Obsessed with Reason Is Going Woo." *New Atlantis* (Spring 2023).

Byron, Michael J. "Catholic Universities Must Teach Faith across Disciplines." *America,* February 8, 2016.

Cacciari, Massimo. *Il lavoro dello spirito.* Milan: Adelphi 2020.

Calasso, Roberto. *The Unnamable Present,* translated by Richard Dixon. New York: Farrar Straus and Giroux, 2019). Original Italian: *L'innominabile attuale.* Milan: Adelphi, 2017.

Caldwell, Christopher. "The Fateful Nineties." *First Things* (October 2023).

Carpenter, Anne M. *Nothing Gained Is Eternal: A Theology of Tradition.* Minneapolis, MN: Fortress Press, 2022.

Chamorro-Premuzic, Tomas, and Becky Frankiewicz. "6 Reasons Why Higher Education Needs to Be Disrupted." *Harvard Business Review* (November 19, 2019).

Clifford, Catherine, and Massimo Faggioli, eds. *The Oxford Handbook of Vatican II.* Oxford: Oxford University Press, 2023.

Chinnici, Joseph P. *American Catholicism Transformed: From the Cold War through the Council.* New York: Oxford University Press, 2021.

———. "An Historian's Creed and the Emergence of Postconciliar Culture Wars." *The Catholic Historical Review* 94, no. 2 (2008): 219–44

Coakley, Sarah. "Shaping the Field: A Transatlantic Perspective." In *Fields of Faith: Theology and Religious Studies for the Twenty-First Century*, edited by David F. Ford, Ben Quash, and Janet Martin Soskice, 39–55. Cambridge, UK: Cambridge University Press, 2005.

Coda, Piero. "Non c'è riforma della Chiesa senza riforma della teologia." *L'Osservatore Romano*, July 23, 2023.

Congar, Yves. *Tradition and Traditions: An Historical and a Theological Essay.* New York: Macmillan, 1967.

Conti, Greg. "The Rise of the Sectarian University." *Compact Magazine*, December 28, 2023.

Daston, Lorraine. *Rules: A Short History of What We Live By.* Princeton, NJ: Princeton University Press, 2022.

Deavel, David P. "The Collegiate Ideal Renewed: Catholic Studies as Newmanian Project." *A Word in Season* (Fall 2020): 57–74.

Delgado, Mariano. "Mysterium Salutis als innovativer systematischer Ansatz im Anschluss an das Zweite Vatikanische Konzil." In *La réception du Concile Vatican II par les théologiens suisses: Die Rezeption des II Vaticanums durch Schweizer Theologen*, edited by Guy Bedouelle and Mariano Delgado, 167–78. Fribourg: Academic Press Fribourg, 2011.

Deneen, Patrick. *Why Liberalism Failed.* New Haven, CT: Yale University Press, 2019.

Dreher, Rod. *The Benedict Option: A Strategy for Christians in a Post-Christian Nation.* New York: Sentinel, 2017.

Eagleton, Terry. *Culture and the Death of God.* New Haven, CT: Yale University Press, 2015.

———. *The Idea of Culture.* Oxford: Blackwell, 2009.

———. "The Slow Death of the University." *The Chronicle of Higher Education*, April 6, 2015.

Ellis, John Tracy. "American Catholics and Intellectual Life." *Thought* 30 (Autumn 1955): 351–88.

Esposito, Roberto. *Instituting Thought: Three Paradigms of Political Ontology*, translated by Mark Epstein. Cambridge UK: Polity, 2021.

Faggioli, Massimo. *The Liminal Papacy of Pope Francis: Moving toward Global Catholicity*. Maryknoll, NY: Orbis Books, 2020.

———. "Que reste-t-il de Vatican II? Sexisme, racisme, crise des abus et régimes d'historicité dans l'Église." *Revue Théologique de Louvain*, 2024.

———. *Pope Francis: Tradition in Transition*. Mahwah, NJ: Paulist Press, 2015.

———. "Theology between the University and the Church as a 'Field Hospital.'" In *Theology and the University*. edited by Fáinche Ryan, Dirk Ansorge, and Josef Quitterer, 39–54. Abingdon, Oxfordshire: Routledge, 2024.

———. *Vatican II: The Battle for Meaning*. Mahwah, NJ: Paulist Press, 2012.

Faggioli, Massimo, and Bryan Froehle. *Global Catholicism: Between Disruption and Encounter*, Studies in Global Catholicism 1. Leiden: Brill, 2024.

Francis. Motu proprio *Ad theologiam promovendam*. November 1, 2023.

———. "Audience with the Community of the Catholic University of Portugal." October 26, 2017.

———. Encyclical *Laudato Si'*. May 24, 2015.

———. "Encounter with Students and Representatives of the Academic World." University of Bologna. October 1, 2017.

———. "Letter to the Grand Chancellor of the Pontificia Universidad Católica Argentina for the 100th Anniversary of the Founding of the Faculty of Theology." March 3, 2015.

———. "Meeting with Students of the Universidade Católica Portugesa (Lisbon)." August 3, 2023.

————. "Speech to the Pontifical Theological Faculty of Southern Italy—San Luigi Section—of Naples." June 21, 2019.

————. Apostolic Constitution *Veritatis Gaudium* on ecclesiastical universities and faculties. December 8, 2017.

Gaillardetz, Richard R. "Do We Need a New(er) Apologetics?" *America.* February 2, 2004.

————. "Loving and Reforming a Holy Yet Broken Church." Lecture. Boston College, September 23, 2022.

Gleason, Philip. *Contending with Modernity: Catholic Higher Education in the Twentieth Century.* New York: Oxford University Press, 2020 <1995>.

Godzieba, Anthony J. "' . . . And Followed Him on the Way' (Mark 10:52): Unity, Diversity, Discipleship." In *Beyond Dogmatism and Innocence: Hermeneutics, Critique, and Catholic Theology,* edited by Anthony J. Godzieba and Bradford E. Hinze, 228–54. Collegeville, MN: Liturgical Press, 2017.

————. "The Anti-Incarnational Affect and Its Overcoming." In *American Catholicism in the 21st Century,* edited by Benjamin T. Peters and Nicholas Rademacher. The Annual Publication of the College Theology Society, vol. 63, 80–87. Maryknoll, NY: Orbis Books, 2018.

————. "Who Is the 'Polis' Addressed by Political Theology? Notes on a Conundrum." *Theological Studies* 80, no. 4 (2019): 879–96.

Green, Emma. "Have the Liberal Arts Gone Conservative?" *The New Yorker,* March 18, 2024.

Hahn, Michael. "The University: The Catholic University in the Modern World." In *Hesburgh of Notre Dame: Assessments of a Legacy,* edited by Todd C. Ream and Michael J. James, 41–67. Cham Switzerland: Palgrave Macmillan, 2023.

Han, Byung-Chul. *The Disappearance of Rituals: A Topology of the Present,* translated by Daniel Steuer. Medford, MA: Polity, 2020.

———. *Vita Contemplativa: In Praise of Inactivity*, translated by Daniel Steuer. Medford, MA: Polity, 2024. In German, *Vita contemplativa. Oder von der Untätigkeit*, Berlin: Bullstein, 2022.

Hahnenberg, Edward P. "Theodore M. Hesburgh, Theologian: Revisiting Land O'Lakes Fifty Years Later." *Theological Studies* 78, no. 4 (2017): 930–59.

Harari, Yuval Noah. *Homo Deus: A Brief History of Tomorrow*. New York: Harper Perennial, 2018.

Hartog, François. *Regimes of Historicity*. New York: Columbia University Press, 2015). In French: *Régimes d'historicité: Présentisme et expériences du temps*. Paris: Seuil, 2003.

———. *Chronos: L'Occident aux prises avec le Temps*. Paris: Gallimard, 2020.

Haughey, John C. *Where Is Knowing Going? The Horizons of the Knowing Subject*. Washington, DC: Georgetown University Press, 2009.

Heft, James L. *The Future of Catholic Higher Education: The Open Circle*. New York: Oxford University Press, 2021.

Heil, John-Paul, and Stephen McGinley. "Core Fellows: Addressing the Catholic Intellectual Tradition's Incompatibility with Adjunctification." *Journal of Catholic Higher Education* 40, no. 2 (2021): 163–74.

Hervieu-Léger, Danièle. *Catholicisme, la fin d'un monde*. Paris: Bayard, 2003.

———. *Le pèlerin et le converti: La religion en mouvement*. Paris: Flammarion, 1999.

Hildebrand, Stephen, and Sean Sheridan. *Fidelity and Freedom: Ex Corde Ecclesiae at Twenty-Five*. Steubenville, OH: Franciscan University Press, 2018.

Hitz, Zena. *Lost in Thought: The Hidden Pleasures of an Intellectual Life*. Princeton, NJ: Princeton University Press, 2020.

Holzbrecher, Sebastian, Julia Knop, Benedikt Kranemann, and Jörg Seiler, eds. *Revolte in der Kirche? Das Jahr 1968 und seine Folgen.* Freiburg: Herder, 2018.

Hunter, James Davison. *Culture Wars: The Struggle to Define America.* New York: Basic Books, 1991.

Joas, Hans. *Faith as an Option: Possible Futures for Christianity.* Stanford, CA: Stanford University Press, 2014.

Kaplan, Grant. "The Crisis in Catholic Theology." *America,* May 19, 2021.

Kaveny, Cathleen. *Prophecy without Contempt: Religious Discourse in the Public Square.* Cambridge, MA: Harvard University Press, 2018.

Keenan, James F. *University Ethics: How Colleges Can Build and Benefit from a Culture of Ethics.* Lanham MD: Rowman & Littlefield, 2015.

Kepel, Gilles. *The Revenge of God: The Resurgence of Islam Christianity and Judaism in the Modern World.* University Park: Pennsylvania State University Press, 1994. Original in French: *La revanche de Dieu.* Paris: Seuil, 1991.

Komonchak, Joseph A. "Novelty in Continuity: Pope Benedict's interpretation of Vatican II." *America,* February 2, 2009.

Koselleck, Reinhart. *Futures Past: On the Semantics of Historical Time.* New York: Columbia University Press, 2004. Original in German: *Vergangene Zukunft: Zur Semantik geschichtlicher Zeiten.* Frankfurt am Main: Suhrkamp, 1979.

Krieger, Gerhard, ed. *Zur Zukunft der Theologie in Kirche, Universität und Gesellschaft* (Quaestiones disputatae, 283). Freiburg: Herder, 2017.

Lasch, Christopher. *Culture de masse ou culture populaire?* Castelnau-le-Lez, Hérault: Climats, 2001.

Luciani, Rafael, and Serena Noceti. *Sinodalmente: Forma y reforma de una Iglesia sinodal.* Madrid: PPC, 2023.

MacIntyre, Alasdair. *God, Philosophy, Universities: A Selective History of the Catholic Philosophical Tradition.* Lanham, MD: Rowman & Littlefield Publishers, 2009.

Mancini, Italo. *Tornino i volti.* Genoa: Marietti, 1989.

Marion, Jean-Luc. *A Brief Apology for a Catholic Moment.* Chicago: University of Chicago Press, 2017. In French: *Brève apologie pour un moment catholique.* Paris: Editions Grasset & Fasquelle, 2017.

Marsden, George. *The Soul of the American University: From Protestant Establishment to Established Nonbelief.* New York: Oxford University Press, 1994.

Massa, Mark S. *The American Catholic Revolution: How the Sixties Changed the Church Forever.* New York: Oxford University Press, 2010.

————. *The Structure of Theological Revolutions: How the Fight over Birth Control Transformed American Catholicism.* New York: Oxford University Press, 2018.

McEnroy, Carmel Elizabeth. *Guests in Their Own House: The Women of Vatican II.* New York: Crossroad, 1996.

Millies, Steven P. *Good Intentions: A History of Catholic Voters' Road from Roe to Trump.* Collegeville, MN: Liturgical Press, 2018.

Mishra, Pankaj. *Age of Anger: A History of the Present from Rousseau to Isis.* New York: Farrar, Straus and Giroux, 2017.

Morey, Melanie M., and John J. Piderit. *Catholic Higher Education: A Culture in Crisis.* Oxford: Oxford University Press, 2010.

Morin, Edgar, and Anne Brigitte Kern. *Homeland Earth: A Manifesto for the New Millenium.* Cresskill, NJ: Hampton Press, 1999.

Neuhaus, Richard John. *The Catholic Moment.* Harper and Row: San Francisco, 1987.

Neuner, Peter. *Turbulenter Aufbruch: Die 60er Jahre zwischen Konzil und konservativer Wende.* Freiburg: Herder, 2019.

Newfield, Christopher. "Criticism after This Crisis: Toward a National Strategy for Literary and Cultural Study." *Representations* 164, no. 1 (November 1, 2023): 1–22.

Newman, John Henry. *The Idea of a University,* edited by Ian T. Ker. Oxford: Oxford University Press, 1976.

O'Brien, David J. *From the Heart of the American Church: Catholic Higher Education and American Culture.* Maryknoll, NY: Orbis Books, 1994.

O'Collins, Gerald. "Retrieving *Lectio Divina* at Vatican II and After." *The Way* [journal of UK Jesuits] 60, no. 4 (October 2021): 87–100.

O'Malley, John W. "Reform, Historical Consciousness, and Vatican II's *Aggiornamento.*" *Theological Studies* 32, no. 4 (1971): 573–601.

———. "The History of Synodality: It's Older Than You Think." *America,* February 17, 2022.

———. *Trent: What Happened at the Council.* Cambridge, MA: Belknap Press of Harvard University Press, 2013.

———. *Trent and All That: Renaming Catholicism in the Early Modern Era.* Cambridge, MA: Harvard University Press, 2000.

———. *Vatican I: The Council and the Making of the Ultramontane Church.* Cambridge, MA: Harvard University Press, 2018.

———. *What Happened at Vatican II.* Cambridge, MA: Belknap Press of Harvard University Press, 2008.

O'Toole, James, "The Council on Campus: The Experience of Vatican II at Boston College." *Catholic Historical Review* 103 (Summer 2017): 508–28.

Pagden, Anthony. *Oltre gli Stati: Poteri, popoli e ordine globale.* Bologna: Il Mulino, 2023.

Reitter, Paul, and Chad Wellmon. *Permanent Crisis: The Humanities in a Disenchanted Age.* Chicago: University of Chicago Press, 2021.

Rizzi, Michael T. *Jesuit Colleges and Universities in the United States: A History.* Washington, DC: Catholic University of America Press, 2022.

Roy, Olivier. *L'aplatissement du monde: La crise de la culture et l'empire des norms.* Paris: Seuil, 2022.

———. *Holy Ignorance: When Religion and Culture Part Ways.* New York: Columbia University Press, 2010. In French: *La Sainte Ignorance: Le temps de la religion sans culture.* Paris: Seuil, 2008.

Rush, Ormond. *The Vision of Vatican II: Its Fundamental Principles.* Collegeville, MN: Liturgical Press, 2019.

Ryan, Fáinche, Dirk Ansorge, and Josef Quitterer, eds. *Theology and the University.* Abingdon, Oxfordshire: Routledge, 2024.

Schloesser, Stephen S. "'Dancing on the Edge of the Volcano': Biopolitics and What Happened after Vatican II." In *From Vatican II to Pope Francis: Charting a Catholic Future.* edited by Paul Crowley, 3–26. Maryknoll, NY: Orbis Books, 2014.

Schmidt, Katherine G. *Virtual Communion: Theology of the Internet and the Catholic Sacramental Imagination.* Lanham, MD: Lexington Books/Fortress Academic, 2020.

Schüssler Fiorenza, Francis. "Theology in the University." *The Council of Societies for the Study of Religion Bulletin* 22 (April 1993): 34–39, and 23 (February 1994): 6–10.

Schuth, Katarina. *Seminary Formation: Recent History–Current Circumstances–New Directions.* Collegeville, MN: Liturgical Press, 2016.

Slaughter, Sheila, and Gary Rhoades. *Academic Capitalism and the New Economy: Markets, State, and Higher Education.* Baltimore, MD: Johns Hopkins University Press, 2004.

Steinfels, Peter. *The Neoconservatives. The Origin/s of a Movement.* New York: Simon & Schuster, 1979.

———. "Hiring Catholic—Hiring for Mission?", *Commonweal,* September 25, 2007.

Tait, Alicia Cordoba. *Institutional Principles for Catholic Identity and Mission Assessment: A Best Practices Guide.* Washington, DC: Association of Catholic Colleges and Universities, 2018.

Theobald, Christoph. "Faire de la théologie au service d'un christianisme en diaspora. Pour un pragmatisme éclairé." In *Faire de la théologie dans un christianisme diasporique,* special issue of *Recherches de Science Religieuse* 107, no. 3 (2019): 497–523.

———. *Un nouveau concile qui ne dit pas son nom? Le synode sur la synodalité, voie de pacification et de créativité.* Paris: Salvator, 2023.

Tracy, David. *The Analogical Imagination: Christian Theology and the Culture of Pluralism.* New York: Crossroad, 1981.

Traverso, Enzo. *Revolution: An Intellectual History.* London: Verso, 2021.

———. *Singular Pasts: The "I" in Historiography.* Translated by Adam Schoene. New York: Columbia University Press, 2022 (original French 2020).

Vergottini, Marco. *Il cristiano testimone: Congedo dalla teologia del laicato.* Bologna: EDB, 2017.

Spadaro, Antonio, and Carlos Maria Galli, eds. Foreword by Massimo Faggioli. *For a Missionary Reform of the Church: The Civiltà Cattolica Seminar.* Mahwah, NJ: Paulist Press, 2017.

Vessuri, Hebe, and Ulrich Teichler. *Universities As Centres of Research and Knowledge Creation: An Endangered Species?* Rotterdam: Brill, 2008.

Weaver, Mary Jo, and R. Scott Appleby, eds. *Being Right: Conservative Catholics in America.* Bloomington: Indiana University Press, 1995.

Winters, Michael Sean. "Three University Presidents' Failure Is an Opportunity for Catholic Higher Ed." *National Catholic Reporter,* December 13, 2023.

Zizek, Slavoj. "Troubles with Identity." *The Philosophical Salon* (May 28, 2018).

Zollner, Hans. "What Does It Mean to Come to Terms with Abuse? Some Suggestions." In *Concilium* 3 (2023), *Abuse in the Church*, edited by Michelle Becka, Po-Ho Huang, and Gianluca Montaldi, 119–27.

Index